NEVER PARTED

A BROTHER'S LOVING TEACHINGS *from the* AFTERLIFE

TERRI LYNN SEGAL

Copyrighted Material

Never Parted: A Brother's Loving Teachings from the Afterlife

Copyright © 2018 by Terri L Segal. All Rights Reserved.

No part of this publication may be reproduced, stored in a retrieval system or transmitted, in any form or by any means—electronic, mechanical, photocopying, recording or otherwise—without prior written permission from the publisher, except for the inclusion of brief quotations in a review.

For information about this title or to order other books and/or electronic media, contact the publisher:
Terri L Segal
Terrisegal.com

ISBNs: 978-0-9996331-0-6 Softcover
        978-0-9996331-1-3 eBook

Printed in the United States of America

Cover and Interior design: 1106 Design
Cover Photo: Kim Colsman Horner

*To my community of family and friends—
you are my life, and I love you.
To life…you are all that ever was and ever will be.*

Contents

Foreword vii

Introduction xi

Part 1: Beginning with an Ending
    1. Siblings, Bound by Love 3
    2. Leaving This World 7
    3. My First Energy Experiences. 11
    4. Other Types of Communication 15
    5. A Personal Test 19
    6. Cleaning Out and Clearing Up 25
    7. Of Guilt and Grief 31

Part 2: Writing it Down
    Summer 37
    Autumn 45
    Winter *(Pray for Love)* 75

Part 3: A New Year
    Winter 83
    Spring. 111
    Summer 127

8. Anniversary 135
    Autumn…Again 143
  9. Virtues 147
 10. Nothing to Fear 153

Afterword **171**

Appendix 1 . . . . **177**
Appendix 2 . . . . **181**
References **191**

About the Author **193**

Foreword

When Terri Segal suffered the shock and pain of her brother's heartbreaking death, she knew she had a choice; she could "suffer through years of grief," or she could follow her own intuition that there is no death. She felt that her openness to another dimension of reality would allow her to perceive whatever might exist beyond the physical world.

Perhaps, she suggests, an unseen reality has been here all along but our cultural belief has dulled our senses and closed our minds. Could death be "a blessing" that sharpens our senses and opens our minds? She quotes the words usually attributed to the Irish poet, William Butler Yeats, to express her answer to this question: "The world is full of magic things, patiently waiting for our senses to grow sharper."

Terri asks us—and herself—what might happen if we could actually accept death as a *blessing* and life as eternal. What kind of experiences might we have and how might they change us? This book is about Terri's journey to discover the answers to these questions and to create a truly authentic life. Again and again she is reminded that she has to trust herself. Through "dreams, visions, smells, touch, and even in song and symbol," Terri is able to communicate with her brother and create a new relationship with him. These experiences allow her grief to be expressed but also transformed so that she is able to "embrace this life with more joy."

Such a journey is a courageous one since there is no framework for it in our material culture. At first there a few people Terri can talk with about her experiences, but as she becomes braver, she discovers others who have learned to trust themselves and also live an authentic life. It is this kind of courage that can transform us—and our world. Just as the caterpillar is transformed cell by cell into a butterfly, person by person we become the magical cells that change our world.

— Betty J. Kovacs, Ph.D.
Claremont, California

Foreword

As an author and researcher, I consider myself perhaps more qualified than most to appraise the validity of Duffy's "teachings" and Terri's mediumistic and psychic ability.

My lifetime research into non-physical reality quantum physics, esoteric literature and the 15 years science research involved in writing my book: *The Paranormal is Normal—the Science Validation of Reincarnation, your Immortality and the Paranormal* convince me that Terri's experience and the messages she has received are valid.

Both her validity as a medium/psychic, but also the validity and accuracy of the responses by Duffy give us all more pieces to the puzzle and increase our collective knowledge to add to what we already know.

— A.B. Scott-Hill B.E. (Elect.)
The Paranormal is Normal—the Science Validation of Reincarnation, your Immortality and the Paranormal

> *"The world is full of magic things, patiently waiting for our senses to grow sharper."*
> —William Butler Yeats

Introduction

I had a dream that I was standing on the edge of the world. I was floating, just above the ground. I held out my hand and a key appeared. It was small, made of metal, and clearly very old. I looked into your eyes and you let me know—without saying a word—that I had the key to all of the doors I needed to open. You led me to a lookout over the sea and we took in the beauty together. I knew it would not be long before you were gone. You wanted me to be strong. We both felt time moving through us and we were powerless to stop this process. You smiled and took my hand and in that moment I knew we would never be separated. And now I had to trust what was inside of myself in order to be with you. And so…I held on; key in one hand, your hand in the other and we looked out together until it was time to say goodbye.

Each of us is a unique soul. We are endlessly striving to grow into the spirit we are meant to be each day we are here on earth. We are miraculous beings who inhabit this earthly plane for just a while.

While we are here, we each craft our own story and weave our own magic carpet. We are creating our life story in all directions, constantly.

When it comes to death, we do have a choice. We can anticipate it with dread and fear. We can suffer through years of grief after our loved ones have passed…or we can choose to believe that, in fact, there is no death. There is only a changing of form, a changing of the relationship with our loved ones who have transitioned.

This then, can be the blessing of death—if we can learn to see death *in a new light!* If so, we may awaken to the knowledge that we don't ever really die. Rather, we are on an endless journey that is in a constant state of change and opening.

We each have the ability to continue to relate to our loved ones even after they pass from their physical form—but in a new way. Our deceased loved ones are still growing and learning on the other side! The truth as I have learned it is that they are eager to connect with us and show us that our relationship with them will continue to take on a life of its own.

If we saw death as a blessing and life as eternal then how might that change us? Perhaps we might embrace this life with more joy! We might develop new insights with which we can learn how to live our lives and change how we relate to our life. We might put the values of love and service first, not last—behind money and power. We might be able to overcome our fears. What a world this would be if we all lived free in the glory that our time is precious but not limited!

Eventually we will each find out what is in store for ourselves once we cross over, but in the meantime we can find hope and inspiration in knowing that everywhere will lead us to the same place—our eternal home.

Introduction

The story I am about to share is true. Writing this has been a work of both love and pain. I began journaling right after my brother Duffy passed. It gave me a focus—a place to hold my grief and it also became a record of the extraordinary experiences I began having starting the day after Duffy left this world.

The dated entries start with the day after Duffy died. I did not plan to write this, but felt compelled by something inside to share what I have experienced. What I have written is my truth as it has been lived each day. These experiences are the most miraculous, mysterious things I have ever known. But they are as real to me as the air I breathe or the desk I work at.

My new relationship with my brother has confirmed what I have suspected to be true for some time: there is so much more at play in this life than meets the eye. I now experience a continued connection with Duffy. I relate to him as he exists for me now; in dreams, touch, smell, visions, and symbols.

I have discovered that how we see our world determines our world and our experience of it. Through this process of learning to relate to my brother in a new way I am now even more convinced that *we always* get what we look for. And so it is important that we search within ourselves and look for what is best for us—regardless of what others believe.

In times of great loss we can feel disconnected and unmoored. Our desire to continue a connection with our loved ones who have passed is healthy. If we have after—death communications or we seek them out, this may challenge our belief system or the beliefs of others. If we can stay open, a new perspective on life can become available to us. At such times it is important that we learn to trust our own experiences—regardless of what others may think.

Part 1

BEGINNING WITH AN ENDING

Chapter 1

Siblings, Bound by Love

I loved my brother more than words can express. To say that I lost my best friend is putting it mildly. I lost my first friend, my first playmate, my pal. As the oldest, I ruled the roost—for a while. Then my mother announced I was to have a new brother. A brother? What did that mean?

According to my mother, I couldn't leave him alone. I was fascinated by every inch of him. I was constantly playing with his fingers and toes. And apparently I was even at times jealous…and bossy! I hauled off and smacked him with a hairbrush in the face once. He had to be rushed to the hospital for stitches. He survived of course, but with a graphic reminder of who wore the pants in this sibling relationship! Throughout the years we got a lot of mileage—and a lot of laughs out of that story!

Duffy is not actually my brother's given name. It is Jeff. However, I had real trouble pronouncing the "J" sound as a child, so in a moment of creativity I called him Duffy. It stuck. That creativity led me to take a pen and write his name on the wall in our house one day. I think my mom was barely able to hold it together as I explained my reasoning to her. I'm sure she was trying not to laugh as she scolded me!

He really had the qualities of this soft and pillowy name—"Duffy"—soft, caring, loving and loveable. He had all of these qualities. In elementary school, he was often bullied, maybe in part because he was chubby. My mother used to buy him "Husky" pants, which brought him to tears when he refused to wear them. He was stubbornly determined to do things his way. He asked endless questions about why things were as they were and to my mom's surprise, his elementary school principal told her that he was a genius! I believe these early influences in part contributed to his drive to excel at sports and his later penchant to protect the underdog.

We spent countless hours together playing in our den. Looking back it was kid heaven. We had a room filled with toys. We had matchbox cars, blocks, Legos, cardboard houses and my most cherished item—a Suzy Bake oven. Duffy must have happily ingested over one hundred Suzy Bake oven cakes, never once refusing my earnest offerings.

In our living room, my father had a row of keys on the wall that we used to stare at and wonder: what did they open? My mother told us they were keys to the hotels in Europe that he had stayed in on business trips, and should never have been taken. But to us, they were pure magic; so heavy looking, ornate and foreign. We sat together, silently pondering what lay behind those hotel doors. The keys seemed to beckon to us and offer us the promise of something mysterious and exciting that we might someday know.

Duffy was usually my willing accomplice. But even when he was not so willing I counted on him! I remember one day when I decided to play Batman and Robin with my neighbor Tracey. We were restless one afternoon, and when we saw that my dad had left the door to his precious gold Cadillac unlocked, well...what an opportunity!

Tracey and I hopped in. I grabbed the brake handle between the front seats, pushed it down and off we went—down the driveway that is. Both terror and excitement filled me as I looked at Tracey's pale white face.

We sailed across the street and up into Tracey's front yard. As I remember we ended up mere feet from her front door! When the car finally stopped, which seemed to take an interminable amount of time, Tracey jumped out and ran for dear life. I jumped out in shock. My only thoughts were of self-preservation. What had I just done?

Right on cue, Duffy came around the corner of the house. There was no way I could take the rap for this! He came over, eyes wide—just as my dad came barreling down the driveway. Duffy was completely innocent, but there was no way I could take the punishment for this! In an act of pure self-preservation, the words came pouring out of my mouth, "Duffy did it!"

In one quick moment, I sacrificed my beloved brother to save myself! My dad scooped him up and an immediate spanking was delivered. Duffy never knew what hit him. When he finally got loose he ran into the house crying—sore and quite bewildered!

Endlessly we recalled that day—always to fits of laughter. We laughed both at Duffy's sweet disposition and at my shamelessly taking advantage of him. He endured being bossed around, betrayed, and rejected as only an older sister could dish out. We laughed because we knew the truth was that I adored him and wanted to be around him always, for I could not live without him.

We stayed close all of our life, through tears and laughter. He kept the nickname Duffy and that is all I ever called him. As brother and sister, we got along unusually well. We could talk for hours and hours. We loved to ponder the mysteries of life together. No subject was too weird, too out there for us. We had a genuine meeting of the minds and we sparked a mutual love of questioning life in each other.

From the day he was born until the day he died my brother gave me true companionship. Of course we did have our occasional moments, but our relationship was as close to an unconditional love as I have ever known. I see now that we were not just brother and sister but something more—heart friends in the truest sense of the word.

Duffy helped open the windows in my mind and I know I did the same for him. I believe that it is that quality of our relationship, that unconditional love, and the curiosity and openness that have allowed me to stay connected to him after his death. I see now, that in a million ways we are and always will be forever linked…

Chapter 2

Leaving This World

Duffy left this world, by means of suicide, on July 24th, 2014. That morning I knew at a "just under the skin" level that he was gone. The night before I had just returned to my home in California from a trip back East. I had gone reluctantly. I had been worried about Duffy ever since I went to see him for his 50th birthday a few months back. He had been very depressed and I had decided I was going to let him know I was going to stay with him for a few weeks. I debated in my head whether or not I should go back East or go straight down to be with Duffy at his home near San Diego. Since it was a chance to see some childhood girlfriends I had decided to go. I was telling myself that when I got home I would let him know I was coming—whether he agreed or not!

And so off I went. I struggled that week wanting to enjoy the company of my friends while in the back of my mind I was constantly worrying about my brother. I attempted to call him several times, but he would not respond. This was unlike him and had become a very worrisome pattern. As each day of the week went on, I was becoming inwardly more frantic. My friends tried to comfort me but I was a mess. With each day that he did not call back, I became more determined to see him as soon as I could arrange it with work.

The plane ride home felt like torture. I tried to call Duffy around 10:00pm, right after I landed. No response. When I arrived home, I realized how tired I was from the long delayed flight. I had just gotten into bed when I suddenly felt something that felt like a shove against my back. It registered just below my consciousness and I remember thinking "that was strange"—but I was so tired I went immediately to sleep. It turned out that in those early morning hours when I felt that shove, Duffy had passed.

The next morning I got up and without thinking, put on a bracelet he had recently given me. I also put on a bracelet from my grandmother Bertha and a ring from my grandmother Lucy, who were both deceased. Looking back, I know now that I was creating my own unconscious ritual. The deepest part of me knew that my brother was gone.

I went to work that morning and immediately started getting phone calls from my brother's secretary. She was worried because he had not shown up to work yet. I was afraid she would try and go to his house and so I told her to call the police. By mid-morning my brother's two legal secretaries and my younger brother Chris were outside Duffy's condominium. They were texting me and letting me know what was happening. For years Duffy's secretaries had looked after him in numerous ways.

They cared deeply about him, and vice versa. They always made sure the office ran smoothly, even when my brother was feeling down and found it hard to work. They had called the sheriff and were waiting outside for the news. Then, finally the worst possible news came. The sheriff let them know that Duffy's body was inside. As I sat at my desk my brother called and delivered the news. I felt like I couldn't breathe. I was trying to be strong for them and at the same time I felt I needed to hold it together in front of my co-workers.

The next few days brought only a feeling of total despair. With my partner's help I somehow got myself together and went down to be with my family in San Diego. I had no idea how we were going to get through this. I just kept praying and breathing.

After Duffy's passing, I immediately started experiencing some extraordinary things. The first event occurred two days after his death. I had a dream visitation in which Duffy appeared. He was beaming and healthy and called me by my nickname, "T". There was a remarkable clarity to his presence.

We were in a small room and I walked toward him, acknowledging how happy I was to see him. He smiled broadly as I got closer. Then he started to fade slowly from the waist down. I asked him to stay but he kept disappearing and then I woke up. Within days after he died I started to have many other unusual experiences as well.

There have been countless reports throughout history of people having all sorts of synchronicities and unexplainable experiences after the passing of a loved one. Interestingly, for over two years leading up to Duffy's passing, I had been noticing many instances of strange synchronicities or coincidences in my life. I wonder now if life was somehow preparing me for this loss?

Chapter 3

My First Energy Experiences

*"We have to continue to learn. We have to be open.
and we have to be ready to release our knowledge in order
to come to a higher understanding of reality."*
—Thich Nhat Hanh

On a September night, some two months after Duffy passed, I had my first mysterious energy experience. I came home one night after work—heartsick and tired. I laid down on my bed. I had my arms out and my palms up. I was crying and wondering, how do I go on? How do I accept this?

Spontaneously I asked my brother if he would like to visit me. I said, "Duffy I love you and miss you so much; I am so sorry I could not save you. Can you forgive me and would you please visit with me?" Immediately, within seconds, a sensation of rolling energy came into my right palm. I felt waves of energy, pulsing, circling, and stroking my palm and forearm. "It's you Duffy, I can feel you!" I said silently to myself. I asked if it was really him. I asked for him to squeeze my hand. I felt a spark on my fingertips and a pressure all around my forearm and hand.

It was a gentle, playful, but strong energy. The thought came to me: "I am not gone, I am existing on a different level. I will always be in your heart, loving you and connected to you, sister."

Now I am a rational woman, and a professional. I am also pretty open minded. Still, this was a stretch for my level of openness and curiosity. I briefly thought to myself: am I having a hallucination, or some form of grief reaction? What is happening here? After this experience, I often wondered to myself, what would others think?

Rationally, I knew that this could be the result of my mind not being able to accept the magnitude of this loss. But in my heart I felt that what was happening was real—a genuine connection to my brother and not a mere mechanism of my own mind.

So yes, in the beginning I struggled a bit. After all, there was a rational side of my mind and there was the intuitive side. One part of me felt I had a "duty" to be rational. But because I had been trained as a professional psychotherapist the voice in my head telling me to be rational was not nearly as loud or strong as the heartfelt sense I had that something very special was happening that was beyond my usual set of concepts and expectations. And although it could not be perceived by others I was certain that what I was feeling was genuine and real.

Amazingly, I have felt the presence of what I call "Duffy's energy" every day since that first time in September 2014. Every day I ask for him to visit, and every day I have felt his energy—with slight variations.

The sensations have variety and depth. Most of the time I feel a rounded, pulsing energy. Sometimes it goes up and down my arm

My First Energy Experiences

and sometimes it transfers over to my other hand. I can "juggle" the energy and feel it go from one hand to the other like an invisible slinky. This is very comforting because it has a quality of reassurance and gentleness. To me it is a tangible reminder of Duffy's qualities.

Sometimes the energy travels over my fingertips. Occasionally I have felt sparks on my thumbs and fingertips. The connection can last anywhere from a minute to 20 minutes or so. As time has passed I have experimented with this. I can ask Duffy to visit or I can call upon him in my car or at work if I am in a quiet and receptive state.

After the first few months, I also began to experience a type of paralysis when I would hold my forearm up as I lay in bed. This has continued and now happens every time we communicate in this way.

After I lift up my arm, I can feel my arm and hand slowly being squeezed and then somewhat paralyzed. If I try to slowly move my hand and arm to resist, then there is a resistance back. It has strength, weight, and a roundness of form. He pushes against me and sometimes jerks my arm sideways or forward. In one instance he slowly guided my arm toward my chest to rest.

The reason that I say it is "his" energy is that despite my doubts, this energy seems to respond to my direct thoughts and questions to Duffy. The more open, relaxed, and loving mindset I bring, the more responsive he is.

In more than one instance I have asked Duffy to let me know he is ok by asking him to move my hand. Each time I ask, I get a strong response. I know this is not a neutral energy; It *feels* clearly as though I am being communicated with.

Chapter 4

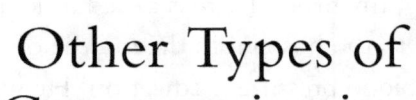

Other Types of Communication

Duffy has made contact with me numerous times, through visual messages, smells, dreams, premonitions, and visions. I have also experienced his guidance through out-of-body excursions. It seems he is introducing me to a reality that we normally do not tap into in our daily lives. He is showing me that our "self" is much more than our bodies. Perhaps he is telling me that once we leave this earth as he has done, we go back to being pure spirit, pure energy—free from a body.

I have had these out-of-body experiences on at least ten different occasions since September, 2014. They always begin with a sensation of my right arm being pin pricked and then slowly stretched out. I feel weightless and then become aware of my "self" above my body. It is very relaxing and induces a vivid sense of peace.

I am not sure how, but I feel that these out-of-body experiences are a lesson coming from him. I wonder—can he change forms whenever he desires? If so, I wonder how that works and how he does it?

Sometimes I have asked him for images or words describing how his spirit is doing. The images show me he is still Duffy. He is still doing the things he would have done when he was here on Earth. He can also do some fantastical things like bending planes of light, as he has shown me.

In one instance of premonition he woke me up in the middle of the night with the words "blood pressure medication." Indeed the next morning, my brother Chris called to let me know that my mother had gone to the hospital in the middle of the night. She had a reaction to her blood pressure medication! He was amused when I told him how I already knew this. Thankfully my mom recovered. She and my brother were both surprised but accepting of this strange phenomenon. They are both open to the idea of us having a sixth sense. They have both experienced it in their own ways. However, to link this directly to Duffy is a bit more than they can take in right now. They are still awash in grief and disbelief at his passing.

Occasionally during the day—most usually at work—I will feel something on the back of my neck and the top of my head and right side of my face. It feels like a gentle touch, like a wave of tingles flowing down the side of my face. I have wondered if Duffy is communicating with me at work as a comforting measure—because I was at my desk when I learned of his death.

I believe all of these experiences are his spirit helping me to find peace around his death. Feelings of guilt are still with me. I hesitated to help him and he slipped away. I am his big sister and I let him down. I was afraid to act on some level. And I had felt fears of how we would pay for his hospitalization or fears he would refuse to go… or worse. Was it these fears that stopped me from acting sooner and more forcefully to save him?

Other Types of Communication

I live with these regrets, doubts, and guilt. But I feel that Duffy is trying to help me with them. Duffy is letting me know that I have been forgiven for whatever I imagine I could have done to prevent his death. This is just what he would have done when he was alive—he would have tried to comfort and forgive me. He would not have wanted any of his loved ones to live in grief any longer than necessary.

It seems radical to choose to believe that the dead might want to comfort us—and can! But why shouldn't the dead want us to let go of our grief and live our lives to the fullest?

Chapter 5

A Personal Test

If ever there is a tomorrow when we're not together…there is something you must always remember. You are braver than you believe, stronger than you seem, and smarter than you think. But the most important thing is, even if we're apart. I'll always be with you.
—A.A. Milne, Winnie the Pooh

Ever since Duffy passed and I spontaneously began to have these unusual experiences, I have only talked about them with a few close friends. Why such self-censorship and fear? My experiences were not anything that I had expected. Nor were they anything that I had been prepared for. So I wasn't sure how my circles of friends, family, and professional acquaintances would react to my sharing these most unusual experiences. I felt I had to be careful with whom I shared this new reality of mine. After all this was not the sort of thing that our society tends to acknowledge!

Those friends I did end up sharing with were the ones I trusted to not think I was lost in grief or madly hallucinating. And I knew they had the capacity to take me seriously. When I have asked what they think I have gotten various responses. Some say Duffy is introducing me to the "energy body", or the astral plane…. or other ideas and concepts. Everyone seems to have a different language for it.

What I do know now, is that in the grief of death my heart has opened to aspects of reality far different from what is usually considered "normal" reality.

Am I really communicating beyond space and time with my brother? This was the fundamental question I had to confront. Either I was experiencing a valid, if new and strange phenomenon, or I was delusional or…? I had to consider all possibilities.

I developed an insatiable need to explore and read what others had experienced after the death of a loved one. I began to devour books on the subject—reading whatever I could get my hands on.

It turns out there are all manner of stories by those who feel they have been contacted by loved ones who have passed. I quickly learned that this is not a rare phenomenon. There is even a term for it now—after-death communication, or, ADC. It turns out that throughout history countless people have contacted—or been contacted by—their deceased loved ones, relatives, and friends.

We who have had mysterious yet real connections with our deceased loved ones are not few, nor are we "crazy" or deluded. Perhaps the deceased are calling on us to share these stories and connect more and more to each other's truth; to spread the word that our souls live on.

From what I have read there are many common themes concerning what happens after death, yet mainstream science continues to reject these. But I believe this is changing. We are an externally

A Personal Test

focused culture—but this is changing rapidly. As more and more stories come out about the unusual and special spiritual experiences everyday people are having, then hopefully these will lead to a paradigm shift in the way our society views the human experience.

As a therapist, I am keenly aware of what it could mean to be feeling things that have no *clear scientific explanation*. For many years I have encouraged clients to explore their inner worlds and listen to their own wisdom, regardless of what others might say. All in all, I am pretty open minded. Still, this new connection was a stretch—even for me. I wondered if I could be having "grief psychosis." Rationally, I know this can be just my mind protecting me from my grief. But in my heart I felt that what I have been experiencing is just as real as the tears I cry. There is a genuine connection to Duffy that is happening. I just have to adjust my frame of reference to accept it!

I have watched clients struggle with fears around how others might react to their changing sense of themselves. Particularly challenging—and scary—can be the changes around our beliefs concerning death. Many people's views are strongly influenced by religious dogma and long cherished family values. Often these views are never questioned until we are faced with death. And then we find ourselves lost, without adequate answers. Letting go of outworn beliefs is not easy!

There is real power in telling our own stories and in learning to live authentically. I have seen the pain that comes from not doing this—both as a therapist and as a sister. In a way, I feel the suicide of my brother was in part caused by his continuing to live an "inauthentic" life.

It's not that he was an inauthentic person—to the contrary. But, after our parents divorced life took a fateful turn. When he was nine my brother went to live with my father. Our father was

Never Parted

lonely and insisted that Duffy come and be with him. Against her better judgment, my mom finally gave in and let him go. So Duffy went to live with my father and my brother Chris and I stayed with mom. Duffy grew up fending for himself much of the time. We visited on holidays and during the summer, but otherwise our lives took their own, separate courses. Duffy lost his two siblings, and we lost him.

Without the love and guidance of our mother, my view is that Duffy got trapped in my father's world. My dad was very focused on external signs of success: flashy cars, fur coats, expensive paintings. I believe Duffy absorbed my father's values, hook line and sinker—to his later detriment.

My brother never had a chance to have his own life and values and I believe that somewhere along the way he became more and more like our father. At one point in a conversation when I last saw him he looked at me and remarked that he had become just like dad, to his horror. I will never forget the look on his face.

Duffy had a strong desire to succeed at whatever he did. He was a dedicated athlete. He studied and became a lawyer, which made sense as way to make money and support himself. However, law was never his first love. Duffy really loved building and designing things. Whenever he was not working he was tending his garden or creating mosaics. He also cared deeply about people and defended those who had been hurt on the job. To defend the underdog came naturally to him.

It took a tremendous amount of work and it was very stressful for Duffy to maintain the lavish lifestyle he led. I believe the stress of this was too much for him. Owning a large home, expensive cars, taking upscale vacations—Duffy led the life of the rich and famous. From the outside we thought he had it all. Outwardly he

A Personal Test

seemed happy. But sometimes we could see that inwardly he was not, even though he worked at hiding it. We were certainly proud of all he had achieved and we are still proud, but in the end he paid the ultimate price for all of his achievements.

Chapter 6

Cleaning Out and Clearing Up

What is life? It is the flash of a firefly in the night.
It is the breath of a buffalo in the wintertime.
It is the little shadow
Which runs across the grass
And loses itself in the sunset.
—Dying words of Crowfoot, a Blackfoot Indian

The week after Duffy's passing was a well-coordinated, non-stop time of action and determination on the part of my entire family. My cousin Brian came from South Carolina and helped us do many of the things that needed to get done, such as cleaning out my brother's condominium. He was a quiet force of strength for us and we could not have done it without him. He was our backbone, along with my brother Chris. We accomplished our tasks with numb determination and worked together without friction. Looking back, it was a truly amazing effort.

Cleaning out Duffy's condominium was one of the most taxing and emotionally searing tasks we had to do.

As I walked through the front door of Duffy's home, I could feel the many ways in which my brother had lived and been present there. To be in his home without him was the most difficult thing I have ever had to do. I tried to make myself breathe slowly, to imagine positive images like dolphins to help give me strength. I did not know how I would react or how my family would manage the unthinkable job we now had to do. This last home of my brother, the last chapter of his life and a place he so loved was now just a storage place. To be in there without him was both surreal and tragic. What made this even harder was the knowledge that my brother took his own life.

To know that Duffy had become so utterly distraught and without hope is to know the truth that no matter how much we love another, we can never truly fathom what lies inside of another's heart and mind. We each can carry only our own self. For some, this weight becomes too heavy. Although caring for Duffy was never too heavy for me, in the end I could not save him from his own landslide. The weight of all he faced—a long struggle with a serious mental health disorder, addiction and loss—was too much. It came crashing in on him—just like a giant boulder coming from above, rolling down a hill with nothing to stop it.

Although we had a job to do, all I could think about was that my brother's last moments on earth were spent alone, in his closet, hiding and desperate. Images of him, and what he must have been going through filled my mind. To stay focused and to hold myself together was torturous. I counted to myself, prayed, and walked outside to gaze at the ocean and to get fresh air. The beauty of the

Cleaning Out and Clearing Up

view from his back porch was in such stark contrast to the scene within his house. For most of the time I participated with my family, all of us scurrying around the rooms, packing up his things as quickly and efficiently as we could. But I avoided going back into his bedroom for almost the whole time we were there.

But suddenly, toward the end of the day, I gathered my strength and decided to go into the closet. I wasn't even sure what I would do there. I just had to go in.

I walked in slowly and looked around at the closet where just a few weeks ago, Duffy and I had sat as he talked with me. We were having one of our heart to heart talks and he was asking me how one knows if therapy is working. My answer was direct and simple—it is working if you feel like you are getting better. When I think back, I know I asked if he felt like it was working for him. He gave me a yes and no answer. But, what I did not realize at the time was that he was really trying to tell me that none of it was working—and that he was sinking. That is where I can get lost in my thoughts; going over and over again in my mind "why did I not see?" I know this is the plight of many survivors of suicide. I was part of that endless loop of wondering how we missed the signs. If I had been paying closer attention, could I have helped mend the gap that my brother had fallen into?

I looked around the space, smelled his clothes, touched his things. The talcum powder for his running shoes had been recently used. The new tube of salve for his cracked heels that I had just given him laid untouched. Everything had the sense of his having *just* been there, living his life and using his things.

I saw the rack of ties he used to wear to court. His taste was colorful and expressive. Some ties had cartoon characters. He still had some I had given him as gifts. My heart sank. I looked around at the neat row of his dress shirts and suits on the hangers. He had a lot of nice clothes but I remembered how he had said to me not two months before that he needed new shirts because he didn't like anything he had. There was the row of t-shirts I had painted for him as well. It was one of my biggest joys; to paint characters on shirts for special occasions. Winnie the Pooh was the favorite.

It was all too clear where he had sat to take his life. The footstool from the living room had been pulled into the closet and was under one of his clothes racks. I sat on the stool underneath the wooden clothes hanger. On the floor was a pile of dirty laundry. I remembered doing loads of laundry just two months earlier for him as a way to help him get organized. He was so stressed that he could not even do his own laundry or wash his own dishes. I had tried to do little things for him during my short visit—they seemed so basic and I remember Duffy saying to me that he had never really learned how to take care of himself. His clothes were pushed aside.

Amongst the pile of clothes was the rope he had used. The forensics team did not bother to take it but had left it there. It was just a plain blue rope, one anyone could buy at the hardware store. I pictured Duffy calculating what he needed and then going and purchasing it. It seemed so sickeningly easy to me. I wondered how he felt when he bought it. Was he sad, angry, or determined? Was he bargaining with himself, perhaps intent on only using it as a last resort?

We will never know. It is this not knowing that keeps the survivors of suicide in their own hell on earth if they stay lost in their thoughts of how, why, what if...

I sat down on the footstool and closed my eyes. I spontaneously put out my hands, palms up and just breathed in.

I felt heaviness in the air around me. It was palpable and thick. I spoke to Duffy and to God. I asked Him to lift his spirit and free him from pain. I sat there for a few minutes until I could no longer take it. Then I went back and joined my family.

That night was a blur. Somehow we made it back to Chris's house—exhausted emotionally and physically. We could see the pain on each other's faces. We didn't talk much—we were all in our own states of shock and we knew that we had to just get through this, and get the job done. The reality of having to return to the condo again the next day was almost too much. We were determined to not let each other down, and to carry on and do what had to be done. So as a family we pulled together in our collective sorrow and carried on.

The next day we came back to continue the packing. This time I knew for certain that I would sit in the same spot and bless that space again.

When the time was right and everyone else was busy and otherwise preoccupied, I went back. Again I sat on the footstool and took some deep breaths. This time there was a feeling of lightness and airiness—there was no heaviness left. I was relieved. I hoped it meant his spirit was freer now.

I imagined I was breathing in sunlight and sending prayers of healing to Duffy. I imagined angels all around him and asked God to please hold him tight.

I prayed to the Universe, to god or the angels, to let Duffy's spirit feel mine and to help him transition. I prayed that he was at last in peace and safe. I imagined my heart had a line of connection going to his heart. I was crying tears of pain and hopefulness that what I was doing was going to help him, even though I had no idea if it really could. Even in his death I wanted to do something for my brother.

I cannot remember a time in my life where I ever felt that there was anything I would not do for him. Of course from the morning he died, I have struggled with the thought that I could have done more. I could have acted faster and yet I hesitated. Was it in the crack of this hesitation that we lost him?

I must have been lost in thought for over ten minutes when I came to and realized I had better get back to helping.

I left the closet and rejoined my family. I didn't tell them what I had done. I wanted it to be my own private experience. I wasn't sure how they would deal with me doing that anyway. Everyone was just barely hanging on.

Chapter 7

Of Guilt and Grief

How to describe the guilt I felt over the loss of my brother? Words cannot describe my agony. Endless waves of conflicting emotions at any given moment would crash into my mind and heart, reminding me that I was powerless before the force of grief.

Duffy took his own life in a most horrifying way. Out of desperation and despair, he exited this world for relief from his pain. I can't stop thinking about his last moments. Was he scared, crying, or angry? I wonder if I had gone to live with him if he would have done it while I was there. I don't like that I had such thoughts, but I did. I was the big sister. I should have known what to do, goddamn it! I should have done more, said more, or acted quicker.

I had seriously considered asking my job to let me take a leave of absence so that I could go and live with him for a few months. I knew how fragile he was. But I hesitated. I waited, partly hoping I would not have to go and in part out of the fear of rocking the boat at work and making a big life change. It also would have meant leaving my partner to live on his own for a few months. Were there other reasons? Perhaps it was just plain laziness or a lack of determination; maybe there was a touch of denial as well. But now it was too late. And now I had to live with myself, my guilt, and my questions.

Duffy left a suicide note for our family. The message he left was raw in relaying the sheer sense of helplessness and hopelessness he was feeling. He believed he had to do this. He believed he had failed at the things he cared about most.

He wrote that he knew it would be difficult for his family, and that we could not have stopped him. We were all shocked by the emotional distance in the letter—we weren't addressed by name. There was nothing like "look T, I know this is going to hurt you." Or, "Hey Chris, I will miss not meeting baby Brian." Nothing! It was as if he was writing a business letter.

The note was the worst thing I have ever had to face. I couldn't read it, and so we had Chris read it. Right after he read the note to us I was overcome with a sense of emptiness. It was another emotional punch, on top of the numbness we were already experiencing after going to his condo. I had the feeling that now there was nothing more for me to lose. I had lost one of my favorite people in the world, in my life. I felt that nothing could ever affect me more or touch me any deeper than this. And yet I also felt compassion and an understanding that Duffy must have lost a sense of the reality of how this would affect us. He must have had the twisted belief that he would be better off dead. I had no anger toward him. Only sorrow for his pain. And pain for his sorrow.

We have a very judgmental view of suicide in our western culture. We think it is a sin, a sign of weakness, of not caring about others. In fact, suicide may be the most viable choice for some who live under conditions that are just too overwhelming to handle. Some

Of Guilt and Grief

believe that those who take their own lives are cowards. What a cruel belief. Duffy was far from a coward. I think that he believed he would always be a burden to those he loved. In his pain and confusion he felt that this was the only choice that made sense to him.

I know Duffy would always forgive me and would never want me to blame myself, but somewhere deep inside I believe I will always take part of the responsibility for this. I know that this is more than just me feeling sorry for myself. It is me attempting to say: look—if I take responsibility for what I believe I did wrong, then maybe I can use this terrible tragedy to learn and grow. I know the answer for me is to learn to listen to myself, my own voice and intuition—and to follow it!

Perhaps it is in these darkest moments that an impulse to do what we must can come forth. Sometimes with separation and loss comes a certain kind of fearlessness. Deep grief and sadness can paralyze us, or it can spur us to action.

In my case, I had the impulse to write what I was living through. I started a journal the day after Duffy died. I wrote in it daily at first, then more slowly—maybe a few entries per week. I recorded my experiences as I remembered them.

Part 2

WRITING IT DOWN

*"Make no mistake about it:
The ultimate goal is liberation from matter."*
—Aghoreshwar Bhagwan Ram

Summer

7/25/14   The first sign that signaled to me that something was afoot, was in the form of a synchronicity. It is just one day after Duffy's passing.

As children, I always used to tease Duffy and sing to him the song from a children's show that we loved to watch, "H.R. Pufnstuf." Singing, "H.R. Pufnstuf, what do you do when things get rough, H.R. Pufnstuf, you can't do a little but you can't do enough" to each other would send us into fits of laughter every time.

As my family was driving to dinner together, I was looking out the car window. A light drizzle was casting a grey sky and a mood of pensiveness and sorrow reflected my grey heart. We drove by an auto repair shop. There on the side of the wall in large white letters was "Pufnstuf". I had to smile to myself, and thought "wow, really?" Despite how awful I felt, a bit of happiness snuck in—it seemed like perhaps Duffy was somehow able to communicate with me!

7/26/14   Last night I had a vivid dream. I was in an unfamiliar small room and I saw Duffy in the far corner of it, across from me. He looked younger and he was smiling and looking at me. His whole body was just sort of floating in the corner. He smiled and said "Hey T!"

Never Parted

I walked toward him, in disbelief and sheer joy. I said, "I can't believe you are here." With that, he smiled and then he slowly began to fade out. I said, "Duffy, wait," but he kept fading. I was left alone in the room and then I awoke.

I opened my eyes and felt immensely uplifted. Later I read about other people having the same kind of vivid, clear dreams of loved ones—which are referred to as visitations. I believe that is what this was! Duffy just gave me a visitation. It was special and filled me with hope.

7/30/14 Soon after Duffy's passing I had a remarkable synchronicity. It involved two wooden canoes and a painting. While we were cleaning Duffy's condominium, I found a small wooden canoe that was almost exactly like one I had found years earlier in the sand in Kauai. His was not weather-worn like mine, but it was the same shape; about six inches long with pointed ends. It was a bit strange, because I had never seen it before despite all of the times I had been in his condo. I had to have it and so I brought it home to be with mine.

That was remarkable enough for me, but soon after I came to another part of the synchronicity. One night I came home from work and was lying in bed just staring around my room, feeling sorrowful and exhausted. My eyes landed upon a picture I had painted over five years before. I had recently placed it in my window of all places, to cover a screen with holes in it. It was right in front of me but I had not really noticed it till now.

As I glanced upon it, I saw that what I had painted so many years ago was a scene of a beach and the ocean at dusk. There on the beach were two wooden canoes— by themselves, with no people!

They were the same shape as the ones Duffy and I each had. What on earth? I had painted this picture years before he died!

Summer

The two canoes, this painting painted years ago…Was this a sign of reincarnation? I had so many questions. Did we live in a previous life together? Did we live on an island and where was it, and what was our relationship? Was Duffy showing me that reincarnation was real? Have we had more than one lifetime together? Do we have more to come?

Once again it was my rational mind which asked these questions and it was my heart that felt enlivened and comforted with the knowledge that this life is but a part of an unending thread of existence. Our relationships on this earth are just one facet of our entire existence together.

8/1/14   Now we're into August and I have had many synchronicities this month. Whenever I have asked for clear signs, I have received them. My brother Chris set up a memorial page on Facebook and it is both painful and healing to see everyone's posts. Often things that are posted there are synchronistic for me.

Today several postings showed up from friends. Two especially meaningful ones were the picture of the Winnie the Pooh shirt I had painted for Duffy and a posting from my cousin—the lyrics to 'Remain In Light' by the Talking Heads. This was a song Duffy and I often loved to sing together and had special meaning for us…"time isn't after us, time isn't holding us. Same as it ever was. Same as it ever was." Is Duffy letting me know something of his experience now, as well as saying hi?

9/2/14   I am on a short break at my sister-in-law's beach house to get some fresh air by the sea. Tonight I ate dinner alone and began to feel particularly sad. I left the restaurant and went back to the duplex. As I stepped inside I instantly smelled Duffy's aftershave. It was strong, distinctive, and pervasive. I asked myself, "Am I hallucinating?" It lasted for about five minutes. I went to bed amazed and when I got up in the middle of the night, I smelled it again. This time it lasted for about two minutes. I did not smell it again the next day.

9/3/14 I heard the Talking Heads song again twice today, back to back, on two different radio stations within minutes of each other. I also saw a bumper sticker that read "I know, no drivers license, no registration!" This was incredible, because one of the last things I was doing for Duffy was helping him to get his drivers license and registration, as he had let them lapse and I was quite worried about it—I couldn't believe he didn't have them.

9/4/14 I was behind a car tonight at the same location as last night and saw the same bumper sticker as last night! Two days in a row! Now, what are the odds of that?

9/5/14 Today my cousin Brian sent a text with a picture of two canoes, side by side, at his local butcher shop. It was a new display. He wrote "synchronicity at the meat market." He sent this because I had excitedly shared my finding the little canoe in Duffy's closet and then realizing I had one too along with the picture I had painted. Brian found this "coincidence" really intriguing and inspiring.

9/9/14 Last night I came home from work and was exhausted physically and emotionally. As I was laying down on my bed I spontaneously asked Duffy to come and visit me. I laid on my back with arms outstretched and palms up. I said "Duffy, if you want to visit, I would like that."

Instantly I began to feel a tingling sensation on my fingertips. Then I got the distinct feeling of pressure and warmth on my hands. It became a feeling of wave—like pulsing and swirling of energy, extending over my right palm for well over two minutes!

I laid still, because I did not want the feeling to go away. I had no concept or explanation for this crazy thing happening. When I asked Duffy to "visit" I didn't have anything in mind, I just said it. This was beyond anything I could have dreamt up.

9/12/14 For the last four nights in a row, I have been asking Duffy to visit. Each night I get very quiet, meditate a bit and then I put my hand out with the palm facing up. If I feel the power of doubt clouding my focus, I then put my focus on my heart and my love for Duffy. I invite him to visit me as much as he wants. I have felt the ball of energy on my palm every time.

It is in my awareness that I have been having some unexplainable things happening and I must see if this can happen again! I know that to share with others what I am experiencing could open me up to ridicule and suspicion. I don't care though! I am going to keep exploring this.

Am I actually communicating with Duffy in his realm or am I just in such grief that I need to believe this? Or is something else going on? The mystery of it is exciting, and not at all scary. My heart believes it is him, and that his spirit is somehow involved in these sensations.

9/15/14 This morning, while still waking up, I had an image of Duffy, sitting down and playing with his shoes. He stood up and he was wearing Dutch clogs! They were the classic bright yellow wooden ones. I texted his good friend Eric and let him know. Eric had given Jeff the nickname "Dutchie" and I know how much he missed him. Eric was so excited and said he had been thinking of him so much lately and that this was perfect timing.

9/18/14   Tonight after I reached my hand out, palm up, it seemed that my hand was being pulled down and outward slowly. I felt a sensation of my whole body pulling apart, with light filling in the separating chunks. I became like a Dali painting, form and space stretching out—less dense than our human bodies; with an immensely peaceful feeling throughout my being.

I felt weightless. I was aware of my "self" hovering slightly above my body with a sense of peace and airiness. This feeling lasted for over fifteen minutes. I was aware of myself in the bed and above the bed at the same time. I have never felt this before in my life. It seemed not so much a direct connection with Duffy, but more of a lesson he was teaching or showing me. It seems to be a lesson in how it is to be on the other side—what it is like as a fully realized spirit free of the body. My thought was that I was being initiated into this awareness. Maybe he felt I was ready to deepen my ability to go more deeply into a new state of awareness. Kind of like, when the student is ready, the teacher shows up!

9/19/14   Today was really hard. I had the deepest sense of sorrow. It was emotionally draining just to get through the day. When I asked Duffy to visit, it took a while. I was impatient and edgy. "What is taking so long?" I thought. I caught myself being irritated with him and realized how wrong that was! Time to re-group, take a breath, and ask him again.

While waiting I got the image of him on a ski lift with sunglasses on. "Is that what you are doing now?" I thought. I was simultaneously angry and amused. I had to smile to myself—it was just like him to be playing at a time like this. Here I am feeling like the world has ended and he is playing!

I hope he is skiing right now. With all my heart I do! Maybe there is a message here for me to heed. He is fine. So why am I feeling so badly? Why do the living grieve so hard and sometimes for so long when the dead are ok? What is the purpose in that?

9/20/14 Duffy visited first thing this morning and stayed around quite a while in the usual way of stroking my hand and arm. I thanked him for the license plate he sent the other day—"GEO EFF". Very clever of him!

Taking a deep breath, with eyes closed, I relaxed yet stayed aware of my surroundings and purposely felt a sense of openness to whatever would show up. Then I asked for an image from him. In my mind I saw his wedding tuxedo. I know how important that day and his marriage was to him. Next I saw the inside of his closet. I saw the pile of clothes with the rope lying on top. I saw him seated with his head forward and an angel was at his side.

The angel was neither male or female. It was a light whitish golden color with some kind of flowing "clothes" on. It did not have wings or a halo as we usually associate with angels. What made me *know* it was an angel is the way in which it was bent over my brother. It was a pose that conveyed ultimate caring, love and guidance. My brother was being lifted up. He looked peaceful and trusting.

I've started telling certain people about my connection and experiences with Duffy. I choose carefully who I tell. I am hoping that those whom I trust won't think I've gone batty with grief. I miss him at times so piercingly, but I know that is normal. I am furious that I can't just call him. I always took for granted that throughout

Never Parted

our lives I could just pick up the phone and that he would be there for me. In fact many times I would be thinking about him and he would call—or vice versa. We had a sort of telepathy.

Autumn

9/22/14 When I awoke this morning I had the idea to ask Duffy for an image—to see if it showed up during my day. It was a kind of experiment to see if he was able to communicate with me through imagery or symbols. The image that immediately came to mind was of a ring—a wedding band. I wondered "why a ring?" but I decided to trust it and go with it. I drove to work and waited for my first patient.

My first patient walked in and sat down. He explained how he had just lost his fiancé in a very traumatic way. As he was talking I couldn't help but notice that around his neck was a necklace with two rings on it.

We talked about the significance of this. He had planned to marry his fiancé just three days after the date that she had died. I was so moved that I shared my story about asking my recently deceased brother for a sign—a wedding ring. My patient was quite moved and remarked, "Well I have two!"

This evening I smelled Duffy's cologne at my neighbor's house. I had promised to have dinner with my 91 year old neighbor. We were having a lovely dinner and for a brief moment I caught a whiff of his cologne. Drakkar for sure! Margie must have wondered why I kept sniffing the air at the dinner table, but she did not ask. It was strong and unmistakably his cologne. Spending time with this wonderful woman has been a blessing and joy through these times, sharing in her wisdom and stories!

9/23/14 Last night I could not sleep. Waking up around 3:00 am, I decided to ask Duffy to visit. I told him that I smelled him at the dinner table last night. Then suddenly, I had a thought of blood pressure medication pop into my mind. I searched my brain for what this could mean. I immediately thought of my partner who takes blood pressure medication. I also thought of my mom. It was clear and matter-of-fact. It did not feel like my own thought and in fact it sounded like Duffy saying it in my head.

I went to sleep thinking that I would talk with Tom about his medication later at dinner. I was strategizing how I was going to say this. The message that my deceased brother had told me to check his blood pressure medication was just not going to go over well! I woke up four hours later to a call from my brother Chris. He said, "Sister, now don't freak out, but mom is in the hospital." "What happened?" I asked. "She had a reaction to her blood pressure medication and her lip and abdomen swelled up." She was going to have to stay overnight.

I have to admit that I felt guilty because my first reaction was one of excitement! Wow, Duffy told me something as it was happening in another place far from me. It wasn't until later on that I thought about the implications of this. This message told me that he knew what was going on with my mother as it was happening and was communicating it to me at the same time. It was so neutral in the way I heard the thought, just three words "blood pressure medication" with no emotion attached.

Thankfully my mom was fine. Soon after I told both my mom and my brother Chris about my experience and how it was

Autumn

confirmation that we *can* know things beyond the normal constraints of time and space. They were happily surprised. Both are very open to the idea of having a sixth sense or a connection beyond this life.

9/24/14 Yesterday, at work when I got in my car at lunchtime, I thought I would try to made contact with Duffy and see if I could communicate with him outside of my bedroom. I got still and quiet and asked for him to visit. It took a bit longer than usual but once I started feeling the waves of pressure on my palm it was pretty strong! I was so amazed that it worked. Now I know it can happen even when I am not just in the comfort of my own bedroom.

9/25/14 Last night as I was meditating around 11 pm I heard the words, "phone message" in Duffy's voice. I also saw an image of a road sign with an arrow saying "straight ahead".

This morning I got a text from Duffy's friend Eric. He had sent it the night before at 11:40pm. It was just a street address with a question mark. I wondered if he was lost at that moment and had accidentally texted me thinking I was someone else who could give him directions. Was Duffy again communicating to me what was happening as it was taking place? I did text Eric about my thoughts and the image of the road sign. I asked him why he texted me this, but he never explained. I wondered if I was starting to freak him out! I never did hear back from him, and not wanting to upset him in any way, I decided to let it go.

In a synchronicity later in the day, I heard the words to a song by Orchestral Manoeuvres In The Dark. It was just one line…"I touch you once, I touch you twice, I won't let go at any price." Later today, it came on the car radio twice! After I heard it, I turned to another station and it was on yet again! Perhaps this was Duffy's sense of humor saying he is indeed the one responsible for the sensations on my hand!

9/26/14   This morning, I reached out my hand and felt my arm being stretched out. It was a sensation of my body being pulled apart and opening up to space. I felt fluid and malleable. I had the sense of being perfectly still, like cement. My body was light—almost as if I was made mostly of air. I felt weightless.

I felt my "self" hovering over my body. I could not feel my body and could not move my arms. As I looked I was able to see down into a deep cavern. It seemed bottomless. For a brief moment the cavern and myself seemed to be one. Then I slowly regained feeling in my arms and body. My "self" merged back into my body on the bed.

I felt extremely happy and recharged from this. This was the second time I have had this kind of experience since Duffy died. I have heard about out of body experiences and these definitely seem to be similar to what others have described. I am guessing that I am being shown this ability because of the extremely open state I have been in ever since Duffy passed.

9/27/14   This morning I meditated and was visited without having to ask. I felt a soft stroking pressure on my right hand as I sat. I have been thinking about my father so much more since Duffy passed. They shared many of the same challenges: mental health issues, addiction, pain and suffering, and depression. I decided to experiment and see if I could somehow connect to my dad as well. We had a very close relationship and so I asked for my dad to come to me.

I put out my left hand as well as my right. Thinking that my right hand is sort of "reserved" for Duffy, I imagined my dad could use my left hand. The same sensation started to occur on both hands! For two or three thrilling minutes I felt both hands pulsing and caressed with energy.

Today I thought about our assumptions about reality and the nature of life. What is real? Is it what is seen or heard and verifiable by our senses and by others? And what about what is not seen, but felt? The sensations I am feeling are invisible to others yet very real to me. I wonder if there is any way of measuring them; of quantifying the energy I feel.

The unseen is not easily provable by science. To dare to believe in things unseen has a long history of being considered by the mainstream as dangerous or crazy. We even have a word for labeling experiences that cannot be measured or perceived by others—hallucinatory. Yet, as our loved ones reach out to us, some of us *can* feel them—and it is comforting!

9/28/14 This morning I felt a squeeze on my fingers and a spark on my wrist and forearm. I brought my arm and hand in closer. I made my hand into a small cup shape. I could feel the pulsing, swirling energy inside. Then I felt a pressure higher up on my arm, like a weight resting on it. Opening my hand up more seemed to allow me to feel a soft round energy, about the size of a baby's head in my palm. After a few minutes, I could feel the energy leaving my hand and floating upward in small bits. As it floated up and away from my hand, I clearly got the image of waves or particles floating upward. They were tiny and light filled.

9/29/14 It has happened for a few days now that when I meditate I feel Duffy's energy come up, without specifically inviting him to appear. It is strong and it can travel from hand to hand. I am asking myself at this point, is Duffy involved in this? Why did I get the same palpable feelings without inviting him? Is meditation a kind of doorway to being able to tap into this energy?

Maybe this is something else entirely and not even connected to him? Where is this coming from? Is it from outside of myself or did I create this? Is this possibly some form of biofeedback?

I am still trying to bring some rational thinking to this mystery. These new sensations do follow the established new connections; they are similar and they happen in a closely connected time frame. Could it be just my own hypersensitivity creating these feelings? If so, why would my own mind create something that is comforting? Is it just for survival, producing hope? Perhaps.

But what I really think is that these phenomena are part of multiple or simultaneous truths, so to speak, that happen when I meditate. Duffy is part of this and he is ushering me into new experiences and knowledge.

I have to smile because if I was delusional or psychotic then I would not be entertaining these options—or so I assure myself. Whew, I must be sane after all! Questions aside, I continue to be open to these experiences and am curious to see what happens next!

9/30/14   This morning I felt a really strong pressure and weight on my hand and arm. It was the strongest so far. I encouraged him to keep showing me more.

I am learning to trust this process and do not have to formally ask Duffy to visit me anymore. I think it is still polite to ask, because I think he is probably busy on the other side, but I see now that I don't really have to ask. I feel more confidence in this new connection; and there is less grasping for reassurance that he is there.

Autumn

10/3/14   Tonight I meditated for quite some time. It had been a long day and I was mentally spent, but as I meditated I felt a surge of energy come in. I put both hands out palms up. The energy went back and forth between my palms like a slinky. I could toss it in the air and sort of juggle it. There was a playfulness to this energy—a give and take of sorts.

I sometimes wonder what this energy is, exactly. To be honest, my sense is that none of us really knows for certain. Frankly we are all in the same boat in trying to puzzle out this interesting, baffling, mysterious, wonderful world. Somehow I have been given a ring side seat to the mystery. And I take comfort in knowing I am not alone in this.

The truth is that I am now in a situation where I am experiencing something so brand new, so different from my usual life that my questions and my best guess answers go hand in hand. I really have no idea what this energy is, but I can feel it and when I do I also feel a connection to Duffy along with a sense of love and peace. And that's good enough for me!

10/5/14   I had another out-of-body experience this morning. I asked for a quick trip and I got it! First I felt small electrical charges on my fingertips. Then my hand and arm became stiff. Finally I felt my conscious self separate from my body and hover just above it.

I was pure, clear presence, weightless and detached. I floated freely above my body. I felt calm and relaxed. After about fifteen minutes, I had the thought that maybe the way back into my body was through my head and down my spine. So I imagined myself entering my body through the top of my head. As I did this, I saw an image and had a sensation of something like droplets or snowflakes of energy gently coming down from above and going into me. Gradually I merged more and more fully back into my body. After about four minutes I was fully back.

I then felt myself moving from side to side like a wave; stretching longer and bigger. I had the knowledge that I was a wave of energy—light and flexible. The next thing I knew I looked at my hand and then felt my body get hard and I saw myself as a statue. There seemed to be no air or space in between any of my body's cells. I had the sense of being perfectly still and dense, like cement.

After this I asked for an image to help me gain an even greater understanding of what Duffy is experiencing. I got the image of Duffy sitting on the stool in his closet. He was having his face or rather a type of mask of his face pulled off by a hand. The hand was not attached to a person but rather a presence. Underneath his face was a ball of light. There was such a feeling of peace and expansion around him. I think Duffy is trying to show me that our bodies are merely the masks we inhabit in this life and that the reality of who we are is pure light!

Duffy has introduced me to this whole new world of energy and subtle body experiences and now I feel like a wizard's apprentice. I am playing with this newfound knowledge. Thank you Duffy for leading me into this new realm!

10/6/14 I had another out-of-body experience today! At first I had a new sensation— the little finger on my right hand being wiggled. It felt like someone else's finger was touching mine; it was so specific and there was clear pressure. Then I had the stiffness in my hand, which I now know means I will shift into an out-of-body experience. I sensed my right arm being gently stretched out very far from my body.

Autumn

As I was being stretched I was becoming more weightless and filled with space. I then felt still and calm with a profound sense of peace and happiness. A smile slowly came to my lips. I stayed in this still and peaceful space for what seemed to be about five minutes.

I then again felt a pressure and weight on my little finger. It seemed my hand was being pushed into the bed. I felt tingling on my fingertips. I could not move my arm even though I tried really hard! I again had the sense of swaying back and forth and this time I got the image of myself as a flag. I am very thin, light and flowing in the air. After about five minutes I returned to my body. Thank you Duffy, I thought. I love you so much!

10/8/14 Yesterday while at work, I again tried to see if I could make contact with Duffy at my office. I did some deep breathing exercises and then I felt a new sensation. I sat on the edge of the couch and closed my eyes. I put my hands and arms out to the side, and as usual I got the sensation of a strong pressure on my forearm. It felt like fingers pressing down on a pressure point on the outside of my right forearm. The pressure went up my forearm almost to my elbow and then stopped. Then my whole right arm was slowly pushed down toward the floor.

There was a lot of strength! I tried resisting for fun and lifting my arm and could not.

This is the strongest force I have felt yet. I lowered my arm toward the floor and felt the energy at about ankle level. At floor level I could feel the rounded ball of energy in the palm of my hand and it had great weight. As I lifted my arm the energy seemed to feel a bit lighter in my hand. At waist level I shook out my hands. A feeling of playfulness came upon me. This was very successful!

Last night I had the most intense experience; and I have to admit it was also kind of scary at first. I was in my bed, half awake and I felt the bottom of my bed being pushed down. It was as if a child was jumping up and down on the mattress. It was rocking the entire bed and seemed designed to get me to take a look. It was unsettling and startling.

I turned over to see what was going on. In my dark room I saw up in the corner of the ceiling, a patch of bright lights!

They were bright, fiery and flickering and flashing with a variety of rainbow colors. I watched for what seemed just a short time. It stopped as suddenly as it started and my room was dark again. There were no more lights and no more sensation of someone jumping on the bed.

I reached out my hand and asked Duffy to visit and let him know that what I had just experienced kind of scared me. I asked him if he could let me know if that was him.

My palm filled with gentle stroking.

My forearm again felt a pressure applied and my arm became stiff. I felt my arm being stretched out from my body, as I have felt before, gently and slowly. It seems I was stretched very long. I then felt a deep sense of peace and safety.

I received the image of Winnie the Pooh reaching his hand out to Piglet. I had to smile as Winnie the Pooh was Duffy's favorite children's book character and I often painted shirts with Winnie the Pooh scenes on them for him.

I interpreted that to mean he was reassuring me that there was nothing to fear and it was his spirit displaying his playfulness

10/9/14 This morning I asked for a visit and put out my left hand instead of my right, just to see what would happen. It seemed that the contact was fainter. The energy was there but lighter, so I switched back to my right arm. Immediately I felt a strong pressure on my hand and then slowly pressing down on my wrist and up my forearm along the outside edge. My arm then went stiff again.

I again felt like I was being stretched out and my whole body and self felt very thin and flowing. I felt like I was swaying back and forth and floating high up in the air like a kite. It seemed to last for about 5 minutes. I then felt a tingling electric spark on my forearm and outer palm and fingertips. After that I could move my arm again. Even though this lasts just a few minutes I feel a deep sense of rest and rejuvenation each time. It is such a counter balance to the heaviness of the grief I am feeling in every bone of my body. I wonder what is the mysterious source of this healing?

10/11/14 This morning I felt the energy ball on my right hand while in the car. I was thinking about an old friend, who knew Duffy. For experimentation's sake, I invited this old dear friend to visit. My friend had also taken his own life about four years ago. He was a sensitive, caring soul who had also suffered with depression and addiction. His suicide had rocked my world as well. I held up my left hand to see if he would "reach" me on it. I soon felt gentle energy strokes on my left hand. They had a different quality to them than the ones I usually feel on the right hand. These were of a softer quality—gentler, and with a different rhythm. I thought this was very interesting—I really have somehow "reserved" the right hand for Duffy to come in on.

I feel as if I am becoming more comfortable with trying to connect to other people, in addition to Duffy. Clearly my connection with Duffy has been a catalyst of sorts and a teacher.

What I am starting to understand is that If we can connect with one person whom we love then we can connect with any person we have loved. I think the love part is the crucial element. We need that positive emotional connection to make contact. I think with a strong emotional connection, the absence of anger that might block this connection and a quiet meditative state, then we can actually reach across the veil and make contact with our deceased loved ones.

10/12/14 The morning today was so beautiful—sunny with a warm breeze. I am feeling better today. I woke up and asked for prayers for my family and for Duffy's peace, because last night really put me to the test. I had been struggling the past few days with guilt and sorrow. So last night I asked Duffy to visit and when he did I repeatedly asked him questions. I felt angry and restless. I asked if he was in a better place, happier, at peace. I told him I was so sad about his pain and how badly I felt because I should have seen he could not ask for help. I was anxious and desperate in my attempts to keep him visiting. It felt like the energy was fading in and out and so I kept pleading for him to come back. In what felt like a gesture of reassurance I felt my fingers being pushed to curl down toward my palm; as if he was saying "let's take a break and rest now." After that I was finally able to relax and slept much better.

After getting up I meditated outside and invited Duffy to visit again. The energy came swiftly into both of my outstretched palms. It was strong and round and soft again like two tennis balls. I played with this energy, bouncing it up and down and side to side between my hands. I asked if it really was him and not something else here with me. I asked that he press down to confirm. Indeed a strong pressure on my right hand and right arm came immediately.

10/13/14 This morning while still in bed I had a visit as soon as I asked. I watched my right hand this time as the energy ball

Autumn

was swirling in it. I could see my fingers ever so slightly moving at the tips. I could also see a slight indentation on the outside of my palm. This was also true of my arm just below the wrist. I could actually see a pulsing beneath my skin. I felt relaxed and at ease. I also felt some sparks of energy on my outer palm and forearm and outer forearm.

This sent me into another out-of-body experience for a short time. I experienced weightlessness and a sense of flying. It was unlike anything else so far I have felt. It was almost as if I had wings. It lasted about a minute.

I said a prayer to God for Duffy's healing, protection and growth. As I did the energy ball was active again in my hand. It seems he is letting me know it is a good thing when I pray for him. I asked him if it was and to let me know through pressure on my hand. On cue, I felt the weight on my hand and arm pressing down toward the bed.

I think I have what the Buddhists call "beginners mind"—a sort of simple approach, and it is humbling. I don't really understand what is behind what I am experiencing. I am a common, ordinary person who happens to be having some unusual and intriguing experiences and I am following them down the rabbit hole. Is Duffy also trying to show me that prayer is an integral part of connection and energy flow? I feel privileged to be participating in this mystery.

I am learning about prayer and I am seeing that it is a much more powerful force than I had thought before. In the past I certainly used it occasionally during difficult times—but it was always accompanied by a certain amount of desperation and hopefulness. Sort of a plea I guess. I think this is probably pretty common with people. We pray for help when we feel helpless or in need of something. But with Duffy's help I am seeing prayer in a different and much more positive light. Positive prayers from me definitely seem to ramp up the energy between us.

> *"Re—examine all that you have been told...*
> *dismiss that which insults your soul."*
> —Walt Whitman

10/16/14 Today is my birthday. I went to my favorite trailhead in Marin—the Tennessee Valley Beach trail in Mill Valley. It is a beautiful hiking trail that I have always loved. I have been doing this walk for over fifteen years. It is as if I can feel the presence of the Indians who once inhabited the land. It is always healing for me to make the trek from the parking lot to the ocean and back.

It is a magical place and I received so many loving gestures today. On the way I stopped for water at the fruit stand. The owner spontaneously gave me flowers.

At the beach I found two roses lying on the sand by the water's edge—from you Duffy? I sat down by the water and meditated and felt the familiar energy in both palms.

I decided to try walking with the energy in my hand. I asked for a visit and I got the energy ball right away. I was able to walk for over 15 minutes with it.

I asked Duffy to give me a present that I would know definitely came from him. When I got back to the car, I turned on the radio and heard part of a new song that has been playing lately. The words "You be you and I'll be me" were on just as I tuned in. Of course! It's the Winnie the Pooh reference to a poem from the Tao of Pooh that Duffy loved. He used to say to me all the time, "You be you and I'll be me." Definitely from Duffy!

Autumn

It occurs to me now that we are constantly given messages and insights if we are receptive. The signs are everywhere that our loved ones are all around us—even if we cannot see or hear them. The most important thing of all is trust. It is crucial that you have the confidence that messages can be received, that you are not crazy when it happens, that your inner experience is reliable, and that you have the inner authority to interpret the world according to your own values and beliefs.

10/18/14 This morning I had a visit. It was different from before—a connection with him on more than one level at the same time. I could almost sense him above my hand, his personality and all. I felt both the new energy and the familiar spirit of Duffy. Then I was led through the sweetest visualization.

I saw each room of our house from when we were growing up in New Brunswick, NJ. I saw Duffy and myself playing with our matchbox cars and Legos. I could feel myself at that tender age of 6–7 yrs. old. I felt our connection in the same way as it felt as a child. I saw each room of the house and the details of each room. I could see Duffy and my little brother Chris. I also saw us riding in the back of our station wagon together and then trading candy at Halloween. It was a long visit—maybe 30 minutes. It was very comforting and sweet.

10/23/14 This weekend my partner and I decided to take some time out for ourselves. We went to a small town outside of the Bay Area to a family vacation home in the deep woods of the foothills. It is nestled among the trees in a wooded area in the mountains and feels secluded and conducive to going within. I looked forward to meditating in this setting and connecting with Duffy in such a peaceful place.

This morning I lit the wood stove in the cozy bedroom of the vacation house and then turned to face the woods outside the window. As I put out my hand there was a small area of intense pressure. I felt my hand and arm "lasered over" by the pressure. It was especially strong. I was feeling guilty and angry about my inability to act more forcefully to save my brother. I cried and wept at one point; I kept saying I was sorry to have let him down. I guess I felt extra sensitive and more emotionally open than usual.

Actually I do believe that Duffy does not hold me responsible for his death and knows that I tried my best—even though I could not see how ill he really was. I am also sure I did not want to see it myself on some level. Intellectually I realize that I am forgiven. But for me it was a seesaw of emotions all weekend.

10/24/14 Today when I asked for a visit, I felt a distinct touching of the hair on top of my head. It was a sensation of someone playing with my hair ever so gently.

I have been able to ask Duffy to visit while I am driving my car by putting my hand out the window of the car and just relaxing it. I try to be cautious. I can feel him just as strongly in my car as at home and away. It is amusing to imagine the other drivers looking over and wondering what the heck this lady is doing with her arm out. I have even had truckers wave to me!

Some days I can hardly focus on my visit with Duffy, even though I ask for him to come and visit. And sometimes I have thoughts going all over the place and I have to forcibly bring myself back to the moment and strengthen my focus. It's like learning how to do meditation! In some traditions this is called our "monkey mind."

Autumn

Today I tried to do something to bring myself back when I became distracted. I began to repeat the mantra "present moment." As I did this the pulsing on my hand and arm got stronger. I asked that my heart be open to all things and for me to be the best person I could be. I also asked that I overcome negative thinking and feelings. In response I felt a push—quick and jerky—that moved my hand.

It was as if Duffy was confirming that this is the correct approach when negative or distracting thoughts enter. I visualized the energy of the solar system and of the earth coming into my heart chakra area to open me up. Then I got a visual of Duffy at his condo on the beach. He was relaxed and happy. We took a walk to his favorite tree by the cliff side, overlooking the Pacific ocean, where he used to sit every morning. We shared a peaceful moment together.

10/26/14   I am now more able to invite a visit when I am outside of the home. I have felt the energy in the car a few times and at work as well. Today, lying in bed, I asked for an out-of-body experience. I felt a lot of energy on the palm of my right hand—a very strong pulsing. Slowly and almost imperceptibly I began to feel light and bright and relaxed. I briefly felt apart from my body but not exactly floating—just very peaceful. I then saw a flash of white light for a few seconds.

10/27/14   This morning as I relaxed and went into a deep relaxation state I felt my right arm being stretched and at the same time the top right side of my head felt like my hair and right temple were being lightly touched. I had an exceptionally vivid experience which began with a feeling as if my bones were fluid, air filled and light—just purely flowing energy.

I began seeing all the stuffed animals I used to have as a kid. Then I saw my bedroom as it was with my doll collection, and in particular, a pair of female dolls who had elaborate costumes from another country. I could clearly see the bright red and white and yellow details of the material!

I saw my childhood surroundings—our tree house, swing set, weeping willow tree and the neighbor's back yard with their two chocolate labs. I seemed to be in the position of being there and being a child and seeing from the point of view I had as a child. I sat on the swing.

This brought tears to my eyes as Duffy and I spent many happy times on that swing set. As I was getting tearful I felt my right arm being gently pressed—as if Duffy was telling me it was ok to cry. I was aware the whole time of being in my room here and yet seeing the childhood scene at the same time. I felt both comforted and in awe that I could see and feel all of this.

10/30/14 This week I feel like I am incorporating the new reality of my relationship with Duffy even more into my daily life. The shift from being able to see, talk and feel his presence in the old, familiar way to this new contact is strange and somehow not strange at the same time. Intuitively I recognize now that Duffy's spirit is trying to help me look forward, not behind. He is showing me how to live more fully in the moment with eyes and heart facing forward in acceptance of life's constant flow. Maybe he is showing me that the reality of existence is that there is no loss, per se, only a change of form.

Of course the times when I do not fully embrace this are the times when I still struggle with acceptance of the fact that he is really gone. Often I wonder what his internal experience was really like in his intense struggle with mental illness. We did not talk about it, really, until the end of his life. By then he was so ashamed. He only told me that he often felt like one half of him could not trust the other half. He was often having a battle in his head, and when he was down, he could feel the "meaner, sicker side" winning. He was so tired by the end—tired of fighting his own thoughts. He was tired of not trusting himself and tired of feeling that he had disappointed others.

    This was the part I tended to dwell on. How could it be that a loving universe gives people such terrible illnesses? Duffy cared for others all the time. He went out of his way to help his friends and family. Why did he have to suffer? I think about all of the people in the world who suffer, who are suffering right now. Some are in grave situations and some feel left behind, abandoned, and betrayed. No amount of telling him how loved he was, how wonderful he was, could change the situation in his head. Not even a room full of people at his birthday party could convince him how special he was. My mind goes over and over this. We could not give Duffy what he needed. Somehow it was too late.

    I see in my mind the image of us holding hands on the last day we saw each other. As we drove to the airport it seemed there were no more words to say, no more hugs between us. I took his hand and said "Duffy, do you know how much everyone loves you?" He nodded a weak nod, probably for my sake. We got out of the car and embraced. He had on his cycling outfit. I told myself he would go for a ride with his friends and he would begin to recover. He did ride with his friends—for the last time.

    Then I had a quick image of Duffy's head. It wasn't how he looked recently or like any picture of him. It was more of a hologram that was made of muted beige tones. When I saw him, I instantly felt him with me, just as if he was standing next to me. Then I quickly saw images of the inside of his closet at his condo on the beach; his bedroom, and his favorite tree outside the bedroom door.

I saw objects on his bathroom cabinet and saw him ascending from the seat where he took his life. Then a black curtain was pulled and I could not see anything more.

Driving to work I again heard the song about letting go…"I'll be me and you be you." *I miss you Duffy, so much, dammit!* I thought. Thank you for being with me, for caring—but dammit *I miss you!* Many times I flip flop emotionally from joy at this miraculous connection to a deep bodily grief that I will not ever see him again in this world.

10/31/14 Happy Halloween Brother! This morning was special. I put my hands up, palms facing away from my body. I am getting more comfortable with experimenting. I could feel the energy in both palms and I was able to play with it; pushing it out, swirling it, pressing against it. It feels like a mass of energy that I am interacting with that is fluid, yet has strength and can move my hand and arm. I felt such a great amount of weight on my arm and hand. I also felt the touch on my face and hair on the right side of my head.

Halloween reminds me of us as kids sorting through bags and bags and sometimes two pillowcases each of candy. We would spend hours bargaining and trading. What a great memory of us sprawled out on the maroon living room carpet, with a fire going and candy everywhere. It's funny to think how much we must have eaten!

It has been almost two straight months that I have been experiencing this mysterious energy. It has been happening every day—often at least twice a day. Yesterday in the car on the way home I could feel the energy as a small but powerful ball on my palm.

When I looked I could see some movement and the pulsing on the side of my outer palm.

It seems that when I say a prayer for Duffy, the energy is more active, as if it is responding. And, when I say prayers for my family and friends the energy also seems to get more excited or responsive and active. It seems there is a direct response to my focusing my energy and opening my heart.

Don't get me wrong. There have been many days where I have had negative and angry thoughts. But I have tried to re-direct them and refocus, and have asked God to take care of them.

Why do we turn to God for help? So many of the ideas that I have always taken for granted are not so automatic anymore. What do I even hope for in asking "God" for help? What is "God" anyway? And how could a loving God allow Duffy to suffer like that?

For now my most honest concept of God is that it is a force, the ground of all creativity in the universe. God's ways must be so much more vast, more grand than we can see from here on earth. There is no other way for me to hold the reality of suffering. I refuse to believe that God is uncaring. But I have to admit that I simply don't know for certain.

11/1/14   I ran into my friend Julie today on the bike path. It was serendipitous as I had been feeling blue all day and sort of lost. She was the perfect person to show up. For her there definitely are no accidents.

We talked about the experiences I have been having. I am so grateful for her presence in my life, as I really do not share the full depth of this with anyone now. I am giving bits and pieces to my youngest brother Chris; but I am starting to feel weird about not telling my partner Tom. I feel as if I am keeping a secret.

Julie reassured me that I would find the right time to tell him and that it is ok if I am sensing he is not yet ready to hear it. My partner and I are on such different pages about all this. I know many couples also have such significant philosophical differences. But the death of my brother has brought ours into the stark light of day. Sometimes I feel we are quickly becoming like night and day in our beliefs. But I have to give him credit, too: Tom is open to the reality that he does not really know what happens after we die. For me there is an increasing confidence that we don't actually die. But I know this idea would be a lot for him to take in. Tom is protective of me. He does not want me to get hurt by the opinions of others. He knows that others often have strong feelings and beliefs on these matters.

Julie feels I have been opened up to a reality of the universe that others usually cannot or do not acknowledge or talk about. We live in a culture where we often label people who are having extraordinary experiences as being hallucinatory or delusional.

This type of experience is well documented by many who have lost loved ones. But there are plenty of people who would dismiss my experiences over the last couple months as some kind of temporary grief psychosis. Maybe they are right. I really don't have a definitive answer except to trust my feelings about what is going on. But maybe it is just as plausible that I am discovering something about the nature of life that is real and true.

When I described to Julie that it is as if I'm not just being shown old memories but being led back through them, and it isn't just feeling a sensation but my brother's actual presence, she described my experience as reconciling. According to Julie, my soul is reconciling the past reality with the present. The truth that survives is the love I feel for Duffy. That is the constant thread.

I want to believe these experiences are actually Duffy contacting me. I also believe I am learning to use my imagination creatively

Autumn

and that my consciousness determines my experience. It seems like these experiences have a larger purpose—for me to learn something about our own power as humans, and about our roles in the universe.

11/2/14 Last night I had the most beautiful dream visitation. I was at Duffy's condominium and was releasing a balloon into the air. It was heart shaped and it was being sent from me to him. Others were inside releasing balloons as well. I went outside and walked to the edge of the cliff. At one end of the cliff I could see Duffy riding a short windsurfing board. He was about six feet away from the cliff in midair! The board had multiple sails. I said "Duffy I am so happy to see you." At the same time I was thinking "I know he is dead and I am dreaming but he *is* here!"

Duffy was dressed in his casual clothes and talking about his attempts to master the sails. His voice came through so clearly, as well as his joy at learning, even though the challenges of mastering it were vexing. He sailed alongside the cliff through the air, talking with me and looking at the sails. He was happy and vibrant, and a bit younger.

I walked along the cliff as he sailed and when he reached the end he suddenly turned into a little boy about 6 years old and jumped up and down on the board with glee. He disappeared into a small cloud and I woke up. My feeling was one of pure joy. I absolutely felt Duffy's spirit.

11/7/14 My nephew was born today to my youngest brother and his wife! It is such a bittersweet time, especially for them. We are so joyful at this new addition and yet the pain is felt by all of us in different ways knowing Duffy is not here experiencing being an Uncle.

I know my brother Chris in particular is having so many conflicting and intense emotions now. He and Duffy became quite close in the years before Duffy died. They took some wonderful trips together and shared some adventures climbing mountains, skiing, camping, and generally really enjoying each other's company. They were making up for lost time. Of course Chris did not have his brother around when they were children. He was only four when Duffy went off to live with our dad.

11/10/14 My new nephew is a radiant child. Little Brian Jeffrey has the face of the happy Buddha. I know Duffy's spirit survives in the most beautiful way. I can see glimpses of him in my nephew's eyes and expressions. Looking at his smile I realize that we really are spirits inhabiting a body here on earth. He is learning to inhabit his new self, his new body. His smile is that of pure joy. I have heard that some doctors believe that a newborn infant's smile is merely a result of having gas. How sad, and limiting—this belief that we are merely biological machines!

11/14/14 It's been a few weeks now of connecting in the morning and nighttime with Duffy. It's hard to describe. I feel a hole and a sense that life is less colorful and yet I am so grateful to still have my brother Chris. He's funny and full of life and we get along so well. I have been blessed in this life with two great brothers!

11/16/14 Lately people have been posting on Facebook photos of Duffy's fiftieth birthday party back in May. Such a short time ago he was here and we were all singing to him!

I cannot believe the power of this loss. I can feel a shift inside myself from where I used to feel the grief to where it seems now. When someone you love so deeply passes, it is amazing how excruciatingly deep the longing is from the hole left by their absence.

Autumn

The grief has taken on a quality of being more pervasive in my body—not just in the heart. There seems to be an overall vagueness in me—a feeling as if I have misplaced a very important item that I cannot quite find.

11/28/14   It took a real sense of determination to get through Thanksgiving. This used to be a time that we all looked forward to—being with Duffy. At Thanksgiving dinner my sister-in-law gave me a book that her friend wanted me to have upon hearing of my loss. Her son died 6 years ago. My sister-in-law told me that this woman had searched and waited for a sign from her son for six years. She has gone to mediums and heard from him through them, but has had no direct signs or contact herself. She is inconsolable. The book is one I had already spontaneously picked up.

I would like to talk to this woman and tell her that through my experience, I believe her son is fine—but I don't really know her well enough to say this to her. So many people like her end up lost in their grief. I just hope that through this book my experiences can be an offering of hope to some.

11/29/14   Tonight, as I meditated, I was very sad and close to tears. I asked for Duffy to let me know for sure that he was here; that he is either responsible for all of this energy or somehow part of it. I felt an immediate cradling of my entire right arm from elbow to fingertips. My shoulders were being held as well. It was truly the most physically intimate contact I have felt so far. I am so grateful for this connection.

12/2/14   Last night was a more unusual type of contact then ever before. I have been feeling really angry these past few days.

I cannot shake the feeling—there is almost a sense of a force inside me wanting to expel this grief from my psyche. I asked Duffy to please come visit and to show me something new.

I got the sensation on the topside of my right index finger of a soft, feathery touch. It most closely resembled the sensation of a feather being waved over my finger. It had a rhythm to it. It was gentle and sweet. It was also accompanied by another sensation of my arm and wrist being held firmly. This lasted for just a minute or two. The rest of the time was the familiar waving and swirling of the energy ball over my palm and the pressure points being pressed on my arm and wrist.

I did feel much better after this. I asked Duffy and God to help me with my anger and sadness; to help me be more balanced and accepting.

12/5/14 Tonight I held my hand up and I prayed for all of my deceased family members. I said hello to everyone and asked what advice they would have for me now. I heard from my grandmother to never give up; dad to follow my heart; uncle Herbie to be practical and from Duffy to know that he will always be there for me!

I then felt an incredible amount of strength on my arm and hand. I tried as hard as I could to move my fingers, arm and hand but I could not budge anything! After a few minutes I felt pressure—similar to acupressure—on my arm. As different spots were pressed, my arm began to loosen up till eventually I could move it.

I have realized that my hand is always very cold after this is over, regardless of how warm my room is.

12/10/14 It's raining. For the last few days it's been so dreary. I keep seeing a new image of Duffy each morning. I know I am not remembering pictures. There is a different quality to the image. It is more vivid, more real and present. Duffy always shows up younger and looking healthy and happy.

It seems Duffy is showing me different aspects of himself. Sometimes he is being funny—like the other morning when I got a clear image of him in his furry ski hat.

12/12/14   For a few weeks now I have been having another type of experience. I hold up my right hand and it begins to tingle and then become paralyzed. It's not that I can't force movement, but it takes work and I can feel the resistance. Next my arm is slowly, gently moved toward the left. I usually have my eyes closed and when I open them I can see the gentle movement.

It's clear that when I have positive, loving thoughts the energy picks up and seems more excited. I'm being encouraged to be in that frame of mind. I can feel the message.

12/13/14   We are in Las Vegas for my partner's and my annual holiday trip. Las Vegas is a strange place; sort of hyper happy and deeply corrupt at the same time. In bed in the hotel, I thought of Duffy's last moments. I saw the inside of his closet, his clothes. I could not stop picturing him hanging from the rope. It was so painful but I could not stop looking. I asked if I could take on his pain in that moment; I wanted to remove his sadness and despair. Right then I got an image of my nephew's face. Perhaps Duffy is saying, "you are helping me!" I took in a deep breath and pictured myself pulling the pain from his heart.

I thought of my conversation with my cousin last night. I asked if she had had any contact with her dad after he passed. She said no because she felt there was no unfinished business. It made me wonder if I am having these continued contacts because I need it, because we have unfinished business?

I asked Duffy to let me know if I was holding him back by asking him to visit so much. Through tears I told him that mom and others have said that they believe that I could be interfering with his progress in the afterlife. I honestly am not sure what I believe about this. I do know that selfishly I want the contact to continue. But after I asked, the familiar energy returned full force. It was not just the energy returning—it was accompanied by a feeling that was comforting, soothing, calming. To me this was a signal that all is well and that Duffy is fine with my continued requests for visits.

12/16/14   This morning I saw an image of Duffy standing in front of the House of Blues here in Las Vegas. He loved the blues and often listened to that genre of music. It was such a clear image and he was wearing clothes I have never seen him in but could certainly see him liking—a crisp white t-shirt and casual blue pants.

I have yet to get a disturbing image. It seems this must be for good reason. I am guessing that Duffy's spirit is reassuring me that he is whole and fine in his new state of existence.

It is we here who suffer the missing. Walking around Las Vegas I can keenly relate to those who are wandering around looking lost. Sometimes it seems almost unbearable to take another step as I get memories of my brother. I want to stop and collapse and just sink into the sidewalk. I have to make myself keep walking. I encourage myself to focus on what is happening right now; to keep going in honor of him.

12/18/14   Today is my youngest brother's birthday. I talked to him last night. He is really struggling with the death of our brother.

Autumn

He feels guilty for being depressed because he has an adorable new baby. I tried to convince him that Duffy is with him and that I think Duffy's spirit is so joyful about baby Brian Jeffrey as well.

My brother's familiar, earthly body is no longer here but his essence will always be. It is accessible to me when I put myself into a state of calm, openness and trust. It made me think about how we all have our "ness" that makes us unique. It is not anything that can be copied or faked. It is our life's spirit in this life, shining out to all. None of us is duplicated.

I received an image of Duffy and I together in a small sailboat. We were out at sea. The water was calm and the sun was warm. It was so peaceful. We had never done this together when he was alive. It seems he was uniting us in a place of ultimate peace, joy and connection. I saw us talk, laugh, ponder and just purely enjoy each other's company the way we used to.

12/19/14 I am telling myself that there is no right way to be in grief right now. Although Duffy is an unimaginable distance away, he seems strangely close by. I am feeling his spirit every day. It is miraculous, and yet I also feel numbness and a vague sense of grayness covering everything. Life seems at times more amazing then I ever imagined and so much more difficult as well.

Winter
(Pray for Love)

12/21/14   It is the Winter Solstice. I said my prayers this morning for new life, the seeding of a future that matters and makes sense without my brother. I got still and practiced some visualizations to make contact with him.

I imagined going to a place of comfort and peace. I chose to meet Duffy on the cliff outside of his condo. It was so special to him and to our family. I waited and then Duffy appeared in a navy blue and white striped shirt. I told him he looked good in the shirt and he smiled his wonderful Duffy smile. Then I saw an image of a hippo with a wacky smile over Duffy's head. Then I saw some lights dancing. It felt wild and a bit out of control. I asked if it bothered him and he paused and said no. He said he was getting used to it, meaning his new way of being, his new power of imagining. He told me he was not yet in full control and that sometimes funny things happen so he just goes with it.

We walked to the beach and kicked off our sandals. Duffy somehow got an ice cream cone in his hand and offered me a bite. I said I didn't think I could taste it as I was not in his world, but I tried anyway.

It was vanilla walnut—I could taste it, sort of. We sat and talked like old times. He asked how I was doing. I started to get emotional and said it has been rough and the hardest part is knowing deep inside of me that I could have done more to save him. He looked at me with his sideways look and said "why do you think that?"

I explained how I could have gathered all of his friends together and maybe forced him to go into the hospital. He said it was his life and he had a right to his decisions. This is just what he would say.

I tried to say maybe he made them because of his mental illness; but he said no, that he knew what he was doing. I started to cry and told him that I was so sad that he could not love himself the way his family and friends loved him; to see himself as we did. He heard me and took it in.

I asked if there was anything I could do for him. He walked me back up to his favorite spot under a tree on the cliff and let me know that just being with him was what he wanted and that was enough. I asked if we could shift now and I felt his energy on my hand for a while. I felt a pressure on my wrist and by my elbow, then pulsing and waves of energy on my palm. After a few more minutes, Duffy was saying he had to go. As he said this I could feel a lifting of his energy away from me so slowly and gently.

12/22/14 Today I asked Duffy, "how do you do this amazing trick?" I am getting braver in my curiosity and my questions about this. Is this mysterious connection just for me, or should I be sharing it, using it to help others? I have a difficult time just "being" with this and not trying to figure out what to "do" with it. It seems so reflective of the life we lead in the US; we always have to be doing something. It is not good enough to just "be."

Duffy's response was highly creative. I saw an image of his familiar smirk. He told me that it was similar to how a caterpillar changes into a butterfly. "When the time is right the caterpillar stops eating and spins a cocoon around itself. Inside it liquefies all of its tissues. But what does not liquefy are the cells that contain the information needed to grow the adult butterfly parts. The cells use the soup of the liquefied caterpillar to fuel the new parts of the butterfly that are forming." Duffy explained that death is actually a state of being similar to the cocoon stage.

Plenty is happening that we cannot see and it is occurring in a time frame that we cannot know or imagine. But from this the soul emerges into its next form—the butterfly. Some souls are more adept at connecting across the divide with the living. It is as if they are able to reach through the liquefied state of becoming and contact those of us who are here in physical form.

12/24/14   I had a special image early this morning. I saw Duffy lying down on his living room floor, possibly in his old condo. The room was bare. I realized that he was there before me and not alive. I crawled toward him and was saying "is it you?" His face was covered in a sand-like substance. I said, "Can I see your face?"

As I got right up over him he faded away into the floor. Just a mouth remained. I leaned over this strange mouth. It was very wide with thin lips. I leaned closer and put my ear up to his mouth. I heard him say "what a silly question". Next his mouth went under the sand and there remained just a pile of sand on the carpet. How real it was!

12/26/14   I spent the holidays in a state of constant motion. It was fortunate that we were invited to some parties with lots of people and activity. I knew it would be hard, but I was not sure what it would be like for me. I have been in a semi-numb state and the parties with children were just what I needed. I often thought of Duffy, but it wasn't such a searing pain—more like having a flashback.

It is unbelievable that I am still experiencing this mysterious energy every day! It has been almost four straight months of visits—every morning and night, at least.

I was talking to a friend; one who I feel safe sharing this with. I told her what I have been doing and feeling. She told me that she once looked for literature on the energy body but found that it seemed to be sparse or somewhat mysterious in itself.

The ancient traditions point in this direction. Whether it is called chi, prana, nadis, astral body, dream body or whatever, they all point to aspects of us that are not bound to linear space and time.

12/30/14 Today I started to cry in the car. I could not stop. It was the first time since Duffy passed. I didn't just cry, I wailed. "It's not fair," I said over and over. "How can you be gone and we are still here?

I put my hand out. "Please come see me, please." A soft, flow of energy started up my right arm. As I cry harder it gets faster and there is more pressure—more intensity.

The more I ask Duffy to forgive me the more energetic our connection becomes. I feel the love we share as brother and sister and at the same time the loss of him so intensely. This is so hard!

What does it mean to have faith in God or a higher power or even in "the universe?" What good is a beneficent universe if my immediate path is suffering? I know countless others have asked this same question since the beginning of time.

My default is to want what I want. I want my brother! I asked Duffy what I can do—now that I had failed to save him. What can I do? I hear the thought "pray for love."

Easier said than done. Praying for love means being humble, letting go of our attachments. How am I supposed to fight for him if I just pray?

Winter

But I do. I pray for love and I cry. The energy is still with me, softer but present. It is with me until I get home.

I thank Duffy for visiting me again. Although I cannot *prove* it is him, I believe he has much to do with what is happening. That much I do have faith in.

12/31/14   I feel a battle has been going on inside me for the past two weeks. It's the battle between my feelings of anger, avenge, sadness and frustration versus my faith in love. As I make time to visit with my brother this morning I ask again what can I do? The answer comes in a thought. "Write and love."

All my life I have fought this battle. The question has always been whether to follow my inner guide and trust it or to fall under the spell of doubt and skepticism. Another thought comes in; the real reality of life is the quiet space inside and all negative and fear-based feelings are falsehoods—created by external circumstances. They are not real; they are merely smoke and mirrors.

Part 3

A NEW YEAR

―― *Never Parted* ――

...You opened your hand
and I flew out.

I fly through the sky
With your wound in my heart.

You're the open wound
In every heart—

And You,
It's perfect mending.
—Bob O'Hearn

I am coming to see that we must keep turning inward so that we can reconnect and find the courage and strength to let go of fear—so that we can truly love. We must make the choice to be loving and trusting...despite whatever circumstances befall us.

It appears that my brother died of a broken heart—and I am trying my best to let go of fear and hold onto love. I fear he died a broken man, but for me what is most terrifying is the thought that he did not have to die, that we could have somehow prevented it. It's an ongoing inner battle for me and I have to work to remind myself that even if I had done all I imagined I could have, that no one knows what would have happened.

But Duffy's spirit is definitely responding to my questions and thoughts.

Winter

1/1/15 Happy New Year? I've spent the last few nights in a state of anxiety and sadness. Being sick has not helped. I can't seem to shake my cold. I crawled into bed last night and asked Duffy to help me. I put my right hand over my chest and prayed for relief.

I felt a slight tingle on my forehead and side of my cheek. It moved down my face slowly.

I felt calmer but then burst into tears at the thought of never seeing Duffy again; never talking to him again. It has really hit me over the holidays. I feel a sadness and heaviness that is too difficult to hold. All I can do is curl up and cry.

1/4/15 Last night in my sorrow I said, "Duffy, can you please do something even more dramatic to my hand. I know I am asking for comfort, for reassurance, for proof, again."

I felt a new sensation. My right arm was engulfed in waves of pulsing, pushing upward through my hand and fingers. It was as if my hand was dunked in a fish tank with undulating water all around it. It lasted several minutes. Then my arm was pushed downward toward the bed quickly.

It was so quick. I questioned myself. Did I just get tired of holding it up momentarily? But, my hand didn't just collapse down, it was definitely pushed.

Later today in driving to the walking path I was thinking of Duffy and started to tear up. Right at that moment, a Porsche drove by—it was the same color as his and inside was a man with curly hair and sunglasses. He could have been Duffy's double, his doppelganger. This was more than pretty cool...it was a direct message of LOVE!

As luck would have it my friend was walking on the path when I got there. She could see I was upset, and I told her about the car. With her cheerful, upbeat attitude, she suggested that life is trying to show me something. She said that for her, the *real* truth is that we are all dreaming our lives. We are the dreamer and we are in the dream of our own making. Everything is a reflection of our own perspective, our own personal 'waking-up' story. We are not slaves to our circumstances, but rather our circumstances are in service to us.

To her, many of the gurus and great teachers of humanity have learned to live in a state of awareness of this truth. For them, it is possible to contain the enormous energy and maintain awareness of the human drama without being attached to it. In other words, they have woken up to the paradox of this life. Ordinary people can do this too, but not many actually do, for it takes stamina, practice, and guidance from a spiritual teacher.

I understand what she is saying is that waking up is choosing to see life's challenges as a call to wake up to what we need to learn instead of seeing challenges as a reason to go to sleep, to escape. Life pulls back the curtain, presenting events designed to serve our soul's chosen lessons in this life.

Here we have richness of experiences—emotions, sensations, thoughts and feelings. There is beauty galore, and for most of us there are joyous and happy feelings too which are all part of our normal experience. But of course there is also ugliness and many difficult things: fear, sadness, anger, hopelessness. Terrible things happen to people. People are hurt, abused, suffer tremendously, and

Winter

some choose to leave early. As with my brother, some people arrive at the point where the pain feels like it is too much to bear. Why would a soul choose this path?

This conversation opened all sorts of questions for me, and later I found myself reflecting on her words and beliefs. Who are "we"? If "I" am a "soul" inhabiting a human form, then what exactly is a "soul," anyway? Is it a form of energy, light, or pure love? And why do souls choose to embody within a human form? Can something be learned here on earth that is not achievable elsewhere? And how, precisely, does a soul "wake up" while in a human body?

The idea that everything is the endless expression of divinity is appealing to me. I like the idea that all souls are playing out the reflection of the divine. The loss of my brother has pushed me beyond just being aware of my grief, my thoughts, and my emotions. I am now also aware that a communication is happening that is so beyond what I was familiar with that I cannot ignore it.

Perhaps my soul was ready for the next curtain to be pulled back. Perhaps this had to happen in order for me to get it. Maybe waking up happens throughout our lives, but sometimes it takes a really shocking event to give us the opportunity to see behind the curtain or façade of material reality. Now I see less with my eyes and more with my heart. My life has been one of unfolding to a more pure expression of myself, one that is more loving and more confident.

The first event in which I was aware of a curtain being pulled back was when my father died when I was 23. This was probably my first glimpse of a deeper reality—but I was not able to hold on to it at the time. I had been in California just a short time. On the Friday night of Labor Day, 1986, I spontaneously called him. The conversation was not natural like the ones we usually had. It felt stilted and absent of our usual emotional connection. I was trying

Never Parted

to reach out and say I love you and my father was just barely able to respond with a few short sentences. I felt a distance between us as I never had before.

As I was hanging up the phone, I thought to myself "that is the last time I will speak to him." The next Tuesday I got a phone call from my mother saying he'd had a heart attack sometime over Labor Day weekend. His best friend and business partner went to his apartment when he did not show for work. He broke in and found my father resting up against the couch, on the floor. He had died alone. I wondered how I knew I would never talk with him again, but I also accepted my knowing as natural, and not scary. However I did not really give it much more thought than that. Of course I suffered great sadness over his death and over losing him but it wasn't until later that I even thought of trying to contact him.

Several years after that, I was driving and thinking of him. I spontaneously said out loud in the car "Dad, if you can, will you communicate with me? I won't be scared." About an hour later, while studying at my friend's house, my friend's boyfriend announced he was serving us lunch. He walked out of the kitchen with the very meal my father and I shared many times in New York when I would go to work with him—baked ziti!

When it happened I remember feeling so excited! I didn't yet know about the concept of synchronicity but clearly *something* special had just happened! At that point, it had been several years since my father died. After that I would go on to have other synchronistic experiences that I now know were meant to awaken me to the invisible, yet real field of connectedness we all have in this world.

Then another curtain was pulled back when my house burned down in the big Oakland fire in 1991. My life and the way I saw things changed forever.

Winter

The morning of the fire, I was in my bedroom with a friend. She was visiting from Boston and we had not seen each other for a while. We were sitting on my bed and I said to her "I have everything just the way I want it." As I looked around my room I felt pride in all of my things. I had handpicked it all and I even had my own art studio out back.

I left that morning to go to the city to celebrate my birthday. I was at the San Francisco Opera House and during intermission we came out onto the balcony. From the direction of the East Bay came a wide black band of smoke. My friend Brian jokingly said to me "T, I think your house is burning down." He offered to drive home with me but I said there was no reason to worry. Little did I know I was driving into a firestorm.

As I drove into Oakland, the reality hit me fast. Wind and smoke and chaos were everywhere. I waited at the end of a street with many others who were watching helplessly as the houses right in front of us were on fire. I knew at that moment my house was gone. What I did not know was whether or not my roommates got out or my cat or any of my possessions survived. It was the most helpless I have ever felt, next to now.

It was traumatic to say the least, seeing people trying to run up the street to save their pets and to have to be strapped down to a gurney by the paramedics. That image is forever forged into my mind.

There were many memorable moments in the days and weeks after the fire, but the life changing moment came when I went back to the remains of my house a few days after the fire.

While waiting for the insurance representative, I surveyed what remained of my house. It was only ash and rubble. I forged around and I stumbled upon the space where my art studio used to be. Digging in the ground, I found six one-gallon cans of paint that I had never opened—they had sunk into the dirt. I opened the lids to the cans with a stick, one by one. There amongst the ashes were six round circles of bright color. It was as if life was speaking directly to me at that moment with an unmistakable message. "The creative force never dies!" We are each inherently creation in motion—just by virtue of the very act of living our lives. We may lose things but we can never lose our own inherent power to create.

We can have everything taken away from us and yet our spirit goes on. We are infinitely more powerful than we realize. We are not unimportant or forgotten, but an intimate part of the universe's creative web—and the universe is always talking to us and through us.

Shortly after the fire, I moved to a new apartment that my insurance paid for in a well-established neighborhood in Oakland. The building was older and I felt comfortable there.

I began to have unusual nighttime visits from a presence I did not know. This was the first experience I ever had of sensing another being but not actually seeing them. The first time it happened, I was asleep and could hear and feel someone at the end of the long hallway starting to run toward me in the bed. I told myself I had to wake up and deal with this person. When I opened my eyes no one was there. My heart was pounding.

In later instances, in other homes, I have occasionally felt someone lay down next to me in the bed. I was always convinced there was someone there but each time that I woke up there was no one there that I could see.

I don't know who these presences were, but they continued for over ten years in other homes. However, after I prayed and smudged my room and sincerely asked for them to stop one night a few years ago, they have not returned. Could it be that they were deceased souls who had lived in the homes I was in and I was somehow able to feel them?

Winter

For some time after the fire I lived in a state of disarray. I actually had some Post Traumatic Stress Disorder. I would often forget things I was shopping for in stores. More than once a clerk had to run after me with my car keys! It was humbling. For a while I had to stop working, and re-group. I experienced some depression and even though I had some profound insights from the episode, I was still battling the emotions in my mind.

Soon after that the curtain pulled back again and I knew that I was loved by something more vast and unnamable than I could comprehend.

I took a trip by myself to Kauai not long after the fire. I stayed in a funky bed and breakfast. The owner wore flowing skirts, chanted prayers, and provided the most nurturing space imaginable. Lush gardens, fresh fruit, open air showers and the songs of frogs surrounded me. One day I nonchalantly said that I wished I could swim with some dolphins. Moments later the owner was on the phone, and made arrangements for me to meet some friends of hers at a place called Secret Beach.

An elderly couple met me there, with silver hair, beaming smiles, and completely nude! I was instructed to put on fins and a snorkel mask and we walked out together to the water's edge. Feeling free, I took off my clothes as well. What the heck! It seemed we swam out for a long time. The woman dove under the water and sang to the dolphins, beckoning them to come to us. The man stayed close by me, as I was not as good a swimmer as they were. After some forty-five minutes I was ready to give up. Not a dolphin in sight. What had I gotten myself into?

Then, as I looked out to the far horizon I saw hundreds of fins above the water, coming toward us! By the time I put my head under, the dolphins were among us. They swam all around us, making their amazing sounds—clicking, popping, and screeching. There were mothers with their babies, and pairs mating. They didn't get closer than about twenty feet, but they had their eyes on us the whole time. I was elated! After a while I was getting obviously tired and my escort friends knew they had to bring me in.

When we got back to land I felt as if I was in a completely altered state. My new friends and I walked back to the parking lot. We said our goodbyes even though I could not thank them enough. For the next two days I was just floating on air. I felt completely different—lighter, freer, happier.

That encounter with the dolphins completely healed my depression. Their voices, their energy, and their love healed me. It was unbelievably profound!

Another mysterious experience happened on that same trip. One night I dreamt of a man carrying an armful of oranges, walking toward me. The next day I went to the beach, parked, and got out of my car. From nowhere a young man appeared, with an armful of oranges, and simply asked if I wanted some. I never saw where he came from. Of course I thanked him and took one. But what had just happened, I wondered? Dreaming and asking and then having these things happen in real life was strange, exciting, and mysterious. More of the curtain pulled back.

1/8/15 Two nights ago I dreamt of Duffy in a strange way. I was in my bedroom in the dream and he appeared suddenly. Somehow he looked very different even though his basic body was the same. His face was distorted and almost looked alien-like. I was thinking, "This is not my brother." He said to me "I am like the number eleven, with two ones next to each other. I have many selves, parallel and side by side. I am one and many at the same time in time; it is all happening now."

Winter

I asked who the "I" was. He explained the "I" in all of us is the point of balance, of contact between our many selves. It is like when you see people balancing rocks on top of each other. They look like they magically balance even though their shapes and sizes are very different. That point of intersection is the "I" between our many manifestations. Duffy was smiling. I was confused about what this meant. Since then I have been seeing the number 11 often; another synchronicity.

I have been continuously praying for the light and angels to surround my brother.

Yesterday after doing so, I drove to work and at a stoplight a truck drove in front of me with the words "Three Angels Catering" on the side. All day I heard angel references.

It seems our thoughts and words are much more powerful in shaping our reality than we realize!

1/9/15 My paying attention to the absence of my brother and the daily ritual of asking for connection with him is my way of confronting myself with what is real for me now. There is nowhere else to put the pain—the sadness and utter helplessness and guilt over my brother's suicide—but the connection is a kind of release and a comfort. I breathe through this grief daily.

1/10/15 If I were to describe my life now with one word it would be paradoxical. On the one hand I feel more alive and aware and confident in myself than ever and on the other hand my sadness is so massive that I often cannot get a handle on it. Lately I have been coughing up a storm.

It is as if my body is reflecting my inner pain and I often find myself gasping for air. I cannot take in a deep inhalation or I start to cough uncontrollably. I cannot speak loudly or laugh hard. I am constrained and constricted physically. My main thought is that "I've got to keep going, but I am tired."

1/11/15 Dear Duffy: Your death compels me to send a message to all: "love is always with you! The unseen is real and our hearts whisper the truth."

1/12/15 I talked to an old girlfriend on the phone last night. We were discussing the unusual number of people we know who have passed away early. I remarked that I have had three significant men in my life take their own lives! She asked if I wanted to know how an old friend of ours took his life.

Up until now I did not want to know; especially in light of my brother's suicide. Yet despite myself I found myself blurting out "How? I do want to know, how?" She let me know he had shot himself. It was the last thing I would have guessed. He was such a gentle guy, like my brother and my father. I was stunned. After our conversation I ate dinner in silence and went to bed to think.

I put both hands up and started to cry. "How can it be that three sensitive, kind, caring, intelligent men have taken their own lives?" In the case of my father it was more like a slow suicide—of too many drugs over time. It must make sense on the other side, because from here it makes no sense at all.

I felt the slow tingle on my forearm and then the slow stiffening. I have come to expect this "temporary paralysis" preceding my ability to feel the presence of Duffy's energy.

This time however was quite different. Instead of a "push me-pull you" type of exchange, when I pressed my hand back and forth I felt a distinct form. It was as if a body in its entirety was right next

Winter

to me. It had volume, depth, something more than just an energetic pulsing. I pushed up against this "body" for over 4 minutes. It was astonishing. Is this Duffy's energy body I am feeling?

I thought about how crazy this all sounds. Yet as I thought about that I realized that we usually convince ourselves that something is real only if another person can see or hear it. It's like we need some sort of verification or consensual agreement in order to trust our own experience.

What if the truth is that whatever we ourselves believe is what is real? One can certainly make the argument that even though I cannot see or hear another person's thoughts or feelings, they are still real to them. Our interior lives are only knowable to others through description and yet they are very real to us.

I think I am being taught something important. My learning is continuing. My work now is to adjust my thinking and attitudes. When I am loving and thinking peaceful thoughts the visit is always more lively, more responsive. I believe this feedback from Duffy is encouraging me to develop this confidence more and more in myself.

Over the last few days I have come to realize just how much judgment and anger I have carried all of my life. My family has a legacy of anger and depression. Viewed from the outside my level of anger may seem minor compared to most, but the events of the past few months have shown me the truth. Too often I am quick to get frustrated and quick to judge. I feel a loss of energy and a kind of sadness when I do.

I now pray for peace and love and try to reflect that attitude back in my thinking to the challenges our family faces in completing my brother's divorce and grieving his death. The challenge for me is to hold this positive state of mind as often as I can.

This is not just for me, but for all others I come into contact with. And it is for those generations to follow, too. Duffy is teaching me about love and peace, from the other side. I am full of appreciation and gratitude for this. What a great teaching! What a great lesson!

1/15/15 I am even struggling with thoughts of giving up and saying to this incredible gift I have been given; "you are not real, you are nothing more than my own weakness." But I don't really want to give up and I don't want to be angry. I want to be on a different level. I crawl into bed and I pray and I cry madly.

I know that I am here to learn and to teach. It seems that this profound loss and the subsequent contact with my brother is pointing me in the direction of my path now. "Give me the courage to focus on my own truth, to live it, write about it, and speak it. Let me not be distracted by things I cannot control, or battles I am not meant to fight."

I can feel an understanding of why he felt he could not go on. I say out loud "am I being punished for acting too slowly to save my brother?"

As I say this, my right hand starts tingling and a rapid pulsing and kneading envelopes it. Duffy has a quick response for me. He is saying "I am here" and, "No, this is not so sister!"

1/17/15 This morning I meditated longer than usual. I had a very distinct feeling of my dad's presence. I have been so focused on Duffy and it will be my dad's birthday soon; so I am grateful for this connection with my father.

I felt his gentle spirit near. Images of us together when I was a child came in. I could smell the Dunkin Donuts coffee, taste the donuts we use to share. I felt I was back in time with him as I remembered every detail of his car. I asked my dad for help keeping me on track.

I asked him for help with our family and getting through the loss of Duffy and this finalizing of his business affairs. Right then I felt my arm being gently pushed down and fingers curling in. My arm and hand were guided down to my lap in a resting position. Then I felt his spirit leave. This leaving was the feeling of a light cool breeze, blowing in and through me and away from me.

1/19/15 Last night I had the most remarkable dream. I was in a strange room with my partner and I was dressed in a flowing gown of gold and we were having sex. I looked to the side and see our image in a long mirror. Slowly another figure started to emerge from me. It was another me! I watched the two Terri's interacting. They laughed, shook their hair, and hugged. The two Terris were younger, both with flowing gowns and long curly brown hair.

They communicated to me, without words, that there is more than one of me. My many selves are always in play and each is equally real. I exist in multiple forms on different planes. This is similar to what Duffy told me about being like an eleven—about having parallel selves.

1/21/15 My cousin's wife posted a message on her personal blog tonight. She talked about my brother's death and how it has affected her and all of us. I read it quickly but something stuck out. She referenced people who suffer from mental illness, misdiagnosis and addiction. This grabbed me and I got a sickening feeling in my gut.

Could my brother have been misdiagnosed for so long? Could the real culprit have been the drugs? We knew he smoked a lot of pot and we thought he occasionally did cocaine. We attributed much of his despair to the fact that he had Bipolar Disorder.

But what if that was wrong? I championed him accepting his Bipolar diagnosis. He never did quite accept it and he died believing that no one would love him because of it. Could it be that in my own way I contributed to his demise by not insisting he go to a rehab clinic? For me this was another sickening blow.

I had to sit down. I started to breathe faster and felt faint. If this was true then the implications for me would be huge. In retrospect it did seem his drug use was far more serious than we wanted to believe. And in retrospect it does seem that Duffy had times where his behavior was elevated and erratic. He struggled for much of his life with a mental health disorder and, I believe, addiction. I know that at the end of his life he realized this to his own horror. But he was too sick to think clearly, too discouraged to have hope and too proud to ask for help.

1/24/15 I am feeling so sad—yesterday and today as well. I sat for a very long time last night to connect with Duffy. A special touch happened. I felt my fingers slowly rolled down to my palm, a pinprick on the side of my palm and a holding of my curled up fist.

I am on the verge of tears. I just feel incredibly heavy and blue. It's been six month since your passing and it feels like just yesterday. Just then a song came over the radio…"Let it be." I hear your loving message.

1/26/15 What do I want to say? I want to say that my attempts to walk through each day since you passed, brother, are somewhat rough, not graceful. The only graceful thing I know since you have been gone is my unwavering love for you and my desire to keep experiencing this strange magic between us.

Winter

I told another friend about these curious energy visits yesterday. Without a flinch she remarked that she used to feel her grandmother on her shoulder after she passed. Julia is more open than most of my friends, so I decided to take a chance and talk more freely about it with her. I told her "I am asking for these visits daily and it happens without fail, it's been over four months now." I wait for her response, to see if she thinks this is strange. She smiles and nods, "How wonderful." What a relief that she saw it like that! I guess it is not so weird for some people after all.

I've made some observations. First, this all began when I invited Duffy to visit me spontaneously; it was an innocent, spoken invitation. The visits usually only happen when I invite him. Secondly, it seems that when I ask for confirmation of the fact that it is him and not some other entity, I feel his energy more strongly. There is always a push or a fluttering or a jerk of my hand when I ask Duffy for confirmation.

These energy visits happen when I am in a relaxed state and on occasion if I have been upset they do not happen. And if I get tired they seem to slow down or stop. It seems I need to have enough stamina or strength to participate with these visits. This energy is versatile. It can pull, push, flow, bounce, spark, jerk. It has also the ability to nearly paralyze my hand and arm. On a few occasions it seems to have healed minor body issues.

1/27/15 I went to our local hotel and spa today for a "mental health day." It was time to be in the warm waters, thinking and resting. As I lay in the wading pool, staring up at the palm trees, I found myself choking up.

I remembered how Duffy loved his palm trees. He carefully bought and designed his garden to grow many varieties in his own backyard. He was proud of his paradise. My chest began to ache. After a few minutes a thought came to me; "It is going to be ok, sister."

I felt the pain melt away and a feeling of peace opened up within my heart. It was clear, fresh and hopeful. A string of tingles came down from my crown and over my right cheek. It felt like a gentle touch of reassurance. Then I felt what can only be described as an inclusion of Duffy's soul inside of my chest in my heart area. It was as if our two souls merged.

So this is what the transition from having an external relationship with a person to an internal relationship feels like. We shift to relating in a different, perhaps more direct way and so in death it seems the deceased becomes part of us.

1/28/15 As I was driving in my car this morning I saw two geese flying overhead. It was so beautiful and poignant. They flew above me, in perfect alignment, side by side. I think that maybe this is how I am now with my brother. He's here, now, right inside of my soul. Maybe we are both flying together through time, he in his dimension and me in mine. We are flying side by side, as brother and sister—and hopefully always will be.

1/31/15 Last night I dreamt I was watching the sky and two jumbo jets were flying parallel to each other. Then they stopped in midair and the noses of the planes pointed down at me. I was really scared. I was their target!!! They flew down straight toward me at lightning speed. I ran into the house. A huge flash of impossibly bright light was all around the house. I snuck from room to room peering out of the windows.

Winter

When I looked in my backyard I saw looking back at me a small, grey alien. Alarmed, I ran back into my kitchen. The back door pulled open and in streamed at least a dozen small childlike alien beings. They looked so funny, with big heads, crooked features. They exuded an odd, friendly child-like energy.

I could feel they were here to help me and not hurt me. I looked at one of them—a small girl. She smiled at me and I knew they had been sent to me. I was not afraid and was sort of amused at how they looked. They gathered around me, like children at the hem of their mother's skirt. They were smiling, giggling amongst themselves. I felt some discomfort but amused at the same time. Is this really an alien visitation? Am I being shown or awakened to even more truths? Are aliens real? This dream was so very vivid…almost like the visitation dreams of Duffy. Is he showing me still more realities that I am not aware of? Aliens? It's kind of funny to me and also the prospect is kind of exciting! I have to admit it is all a bit much to take in. I'm not sure what to think!

2/3/15 This morning I was reminded of a dream I had last night. I dreamt Duffy was lying on the floor in a house I did not recognize.

I ran up to him and put my face down next to his. I looked into his face which was parallel to the floor and I said "Duffy do you know how much I love you?" He smiled and nodded and said yes. Then I said, with my face even closer, "do you know how many people love you and miss you?"

He smiled again and said yes. Then his face appeared to kind of melt into the floor with just an outline of the silhouette of his head. I said one more time, "I love you so much." He said he knew and then I woke up. It was so vivid; I was left with his face and smile and voice.

2/12/15   The other night I spoke to my younger brother Chris. He was sad after a day of visiting Duffy's old home and work-site. I could hear the despair in his voice. I hung up the phone and meditated. I asked Duffy to please send him a sign if he could as he really needs it! I saw an image of Duffy looking at me and cocking his head to the side the way he used to when he was really thinking about what was being said to him.

The next morning Chris let me know through a text that he had had a fantastic dream of Duffy that night. I was so excited. Duffy heard me and responded! I spoke to Chris that night. He dreamt that he and Duffy were on some kind of a demolition site. They were adults on the site but then became children and were in a small bedroom as kids. They were wrestling just like they used to. He said it made him very happy. Thank you Duffy, I know you did this because of your love for your brother.

2/13/15   I looked at some old pictures tonight. As I was looking at a photo of Duffy and our godfather Marvin, taken at Duffy's 50th birthday party, I can clearly see the darkness in my brother's eyes. His eyes are dark and lifeless. There is no light in them. It just so happened that as I was taking a notepad out of my drawer I pulled out an older photo of Duffy. He was younger and had just started his law practice. His eyes were shining. What happened my dear brother, what happened to pull the light from your eyes?

2/14/15 It's Valentine's day and I had a sweet visit from Duffy at the cafe. Just as my friend and I were speaking he sent me the Talking Heads song—'Remain in Light.' Perfect timing! For weeks now I have gotten his signs. So often I see visions of him when I wake up.

I guided myself into my own shamanic journey last night using some tools that I have been taught: closing my eyes, listening to a hypnotic drum beat, relaxing my body, breathing deeply and imagining myself diving deeply into lower realms. I received an answer to my question of "Duffy, where are you now?" In the vision I was invited to ride on the back of a young female spirit—kind of like Tinkerbell. She had wings and the body of a young girl.

As we flew she became a butterfly. The butterfly became a monarch that was large with its distinctive bright orange and black patterns. Then the monarch flew up into the branches with thousands of other monarchs. I believe she was showing me that the answer is that Duffy has transformed and is now part of a larger group consciousness.

Never Parted

YOUR GUARDIAN ANGEL SPEAKS

*When I was alive,
I set up plastic saints on the floor.*

*Now I peel skin and
hide it from you to find.
We used to be siblings
But I've become your messenger,
filled with the Sinai and flickers of harp.*

*I know the seeds you've planted.
Your fear of dark harbors,
Your fast driving down fevered streets.*

*Let me remind you that you are divine,
Even as you walk between
the dead and the disheveled.
Your carnival tales rest
safely in my arms.*

*Follow the tracks of the sky.
Hear my yellow, dusty voice.
Trust your bones.*

*Your god is not a seduction:
She's your spirit in silent sand,
a gentle refuge of love.*

—Carmen Calatayud "In the Company of Spirits"

Winter

2/15/15   I have been thinking that it involves a lot of heartbreak to become truly free in this world. There's the pain of knowing your inner self and standing by it regardless of what others think. It means saying no, saying goodbye and giving things up. Loss and death have forced me to go inward for comfort, but eventually, I must check in with myself and see if I am staying on course. But we must also look for it in the places we least expect to find it. Even now I still struggle with poisonous thoughts of anger, fear and hopelessness. I know that when I focus on these emotions I imprison myself. So my freedom is ultimately taken from me by my own doing. Of course sometimes I find it hard to trust that all is well; yet that is where true freedom lives—in that faith. It can be that simple!

2/17/15   This morning I held out my hand in the car the whole drive to work—in order to be with you brother! I am making a point of saying your name out loud which seems to get more of an energy response from you.

On the drive I kept hearing songs that spoke directly to me. The first was *Sky Full of Stars* by Coldplay. This song was popular when Duffy passed and my whole family now associates this song with his passing. Another song, *I Still Haven't Found What I'm Looking For* by U2 really got to me. I worry that Duffy is saying that he is still searching for peace, and is not content. On some level this really has me in knots. Of course what I want above all else is for him to be at peace.

I pray to God that he is holding Duffy in the light. I pray that he is healing him and teaching him to resolve old wounds. It is ok if he still hasn't found what he is looking for. But it seems in many ways he is showing me he has.

From my perspective Duffy does seem to be strongly indicating that he is in fact learning and resolving his old wounds. In fact from what he has shown me so far, he seems to be doing great and has learned and seen that everything is in fact OK and that he is not needing to struggle at all anymore. So maybe I am being overly paranoid by worrying so much about him still—I'm still his big sister, after all! Who knows? Maybe the song was just a song, or maybe he is still searching—which would fit his character—but it doesn't necessarily mean he is in pain, as we understand it.

2/19/15   I am feeling worried today. My blood pressure is up and I cannot seem to settle down emotionally. My feelings have been so intense lately and in such a state of fluctuation.

I remembered how he was planning for retirement and now that has been taken away. The sadness and sense of injustice is huge in me. I say Duffy's name out loud. I ask for the positive, to remember that there is positive here.

This new connection with Duffy compelled me a little while ago to see if I could find any groups or associations that could give me insight or reassurance about what I have been experiencing. I wanted to know if others have gone through similar things. When I found the ASCS—The Academy of Spirituality and Consciousness Studies—I realized there was a whole world—a community, really—waiting for me to share and learn from. I wrote an article for their journal and it was accepted for the May issue! I have a good feeling about it and am proud I got it done. Even in this grief I can move forward.

2/26/15   I think about how I have been feeling lately. I have had sudden pangs of sorrow, like a fleeting wave of nausea triggered

Winter

by small things. Yesterday I felt it when my co-worker and I were taking a walk. He was telling me how he loved warm weather and wearing flip flops. I said without thinking, "my brothers love that kind of weather too."

Then I remembered that indeed one brother is no longer alive and somehow I had temporarily suspended this reality. I also did not want to accept it was true. I immediately felt the air sucked out of me, the blood drain from my face. I had to walk slowly and tell myself to keep walking or I would stop and crumple on the sidewalk. I did not know if I wanted to talk to anyone again that day. I am looking forward to going on a vacation back East in a few days. I am hoping a change in location and perspective will help me feel better.

3/2/15 Here I am, back East. It is familiar and strange at the same time. While visiting my friend in North Carolina, we talked about the death of her father. She told me that she was with him when he passed. She shared that right before he took his last breaths he was looking straight ahead. She sensed he was seeing far beyond her, far beyond the room. "It was as if his body could not take in all of the incredible sights before him, as if he couldn't hold the new horizon in his limited field of vision." She sensed that he was seeing into a reality far beyond the one we normally know.

The ordinary field of vision for us, the living, is indeed limited. Those who have had near-death experiences have come back to tell of their 360 degree perception across the veil.

Here, away from home, I have been able to connect with Duffy every day. He responds when I ask for my hand to be held with a definite pressure and energetic pulsing on my palm. It feels like his hand is up against mine.

3/7/15 This whole trip has been tiring but inspiring! Every night I have asked for a connection and have gotten it. My sense of grief is ever changing. Today it was unstoppable.

I've had so many images of you, Duffy, going through my head. I feel I could reach out and touch and talk to you today. Apparently others are thinking of you today because so many people were posting pictures of you on Facebook. We have all had a wave of Duffy memories go through us.

3/11/15 Last night you were in my dreams in the sweetest way, brother. I was at an old historic hotel. It felt like I was in Key West or Louisiana. I was at the bottom of a huge, granite stairway. Suddenly you came along and scooped me up. You carried me up four flights of stairs without any problem. It was easy and I felt light and happy. You set me down at my hotel room door and then you were gone. All day yesterday I received messages from you. I saw license plates with your name, the note on my office door, the songs and the energy. Thank you for loving me and for showing me you are here. I now know you always will be.

3/14/15 Grief has a will of its own. Waves of deep sadness came over me at work today. My co-workers understand, yet it is hard. This morning as I woke up, I got an image of you and Chris riding in an Ultralight. Chris was flying it with you behind him. You had on a flying helmet and those old time aviator goggles. You both looked like you were having so much fun!

Then, tonight, I stepped outside my front door and heard a whirring sound. I looked up to see an Ultralight over my house! Coincidence? I think not!

Winter

3/16/15 Each day I seem to do a back and forth dance in my memories. I am flooded with memories from before you passed, dear brother. I remember how I prayed and prayed for your healing. I envisioned us laughing at your old house. I asked for guidance and support to help you from God and the Archangel Michael.

It's interesting—the image of Archangel Michael first came to me one time when I was praying for support after my house had burned down. This was curious to me, as I don't really have any particular affiliation with any specific religion and I knew nothing of him. However in the image I received at that time, he showed me that he was a healing angel, a helper of God. Since then whenever I have been feeling particularly low or lost, I have included him in my prayers.

I remember not too long before you passed, envisioning walking through a dense forest and coming upon a golden door. I went up, opened it and walked into a thick white mist. I stood still and waited for Michael. He appeared and he was smiling kindly. He offered me his hand. I asked for him to help you. I then saw him sit down with a notebook of some sort. It seemed he was making all sorts of calculations. I was relieved he was helping and I was sure you would be ok.

Not long after that the signs that you were in deeper trouble began to appear. I still prayed and on the morning you passed I was in disbelief. I had done all I could and still you slipped through our fingers. Could it be that Michael's calculations came up with your passing as the most beneficial healing for you? It doesn't make sense to me from the earth plane. But, maybe from a broader perspective it makes perfect sense.

I still am not convinced though. A part of me feels let down, duped. How could I believe in such a stupid thing as praying to

Michael, an Archangel? I berate myself as I have done many times over the years. But then I think about these amazing experiences of energy that I am having. I am re-thinking my assumption that I was let down. Maybe my prayers were answered—but in a way I cannot fully grasp.

My good friend asked me if losing you and having all of these after-death communications has completely changed my life. The answer is a resounding yes in that I am now a firm believer in the unseen realms and all that they hold as part of the totality of life. Absolutely yes! I have been shown that life is unimaginably vast and extends forever. If we allow ourselves to open the window of possibilities and let the signs come in then we expand our consciousness on this earth. The more conscious we become, the more we are aware of life beyond this physical realm and the more we can move the human race toward love. This invisible world of spirit is friendly and waiting for us to engage it!

3/17/15 I was not able to get onto my computer tonight so I went outside. It was sunset and the sky was bright orange-red. It was the same color as the sky the night of an Italian dinner I had with Duffy just two weeks before he died. The memory and image of sitting with him at the table, just the two of us, took me by surprise and I started to sob.

I felt an uncontrollable desire to pray and to keep saying over and over "please forgive me, please forgive me." I put my arm out and asked "please let me know you are here!"

Instantly my arm was slowly lifted up at the elbow. It rose up to the same height as my shoulder and hung suspended in air. My hand was quickly pushed forward. Strong waves of motion circled my palm and wrist. My neck and shoulder had been hurting quite a bit for several days and I asked, crying, if Duffy could help me. Again my arm was lifted a bit higher and outward. I continued to pray and cry and feel the energy. After just about 10 minutes my arm slowly came down and the energy went away gently.

After that the pain in my neck and shoulder was significantly decreased. This has lasted right up to today and has not returned to the previous level of pain. Duffy clearly responded to my emotional and physical distress!

Spring

3/20/15 Last night I asked for a vision of a healing place. I saw myself in a landscape with Duffy. It was in a valley. First I saw an owl. It was a human sized owl and I could see Duffy's hand poking out from under the wing. We grasped hands and began to fly. Duffy put me on his back and we glided over the landscape.

In the distance I could see a crowd of people. It was a beautiful scene, with pinkish light and warmth. The crowd was anxiously awaiting our arrival. Before we got there, however, we stopped at a fountain. Duffy beckoned me to drink.

As I leaned over I began to weep. All of the sorrow of losing Duffy and all of my loved ones poured out of me into that fountain. As I cried and saw the tears flow into the water and become part of it, I began to feel a steady flow of peace. Duffy told me to drink again. I was aware of the message he was trying to give me. He was telling me that the waters of life continually flow. These waters hold all of our emotions and wash us so that we are free to continue to feel all that we need to feel. There is no judgement toward these emotions; they are all a necessary part of the circle of life. The water of life contains both joy and sorrow. It cannot be separated and in this cycle is the healing itself.

We began to fly again toward the horizon. As we approached the crowd, I could see smiling faces and expectation of my arrival. I could not say I knew these people, the way I know people in my life now. It was more like *they* knew *me*—truly and deeply. Not only did they know me, but they were filled with joy that I was coming home. I came out of the vision just before we arrived. Maybe that is because I am not yet truly "going home." But, I have been given a glimpse of what awaits me. I see there is nothing to fear in death. At the end of our earthly journey we are welcomed with complete and utter joy.

3/31/15   I decided to try my hand at automatic writing last night. I put myself in a relaxed state and guided myself through a journey to connect with Duffy and then to automatically write his answer to my question. Of course I wanted to know how he was. Here is his reply:

I am free! Free to do what I can. You are also free to see me, hear me, touch me. We are together always—there is no separation; only space of another nature—not a wall but a thin membrane that can't be crossed over now. I am fine. I feel good, healthy, strong, in good shape and light at the same time. I have more than friends, they are my spirit family. They help me know what to try next. It is all about trying new things and going forward into the unknown with a felt, known purpose. We are supposed to make whole the parts of ourselves that need work. It is all for the best. I love you so much sister.

4/13/15   A few mornings ago I had a very specific image. It was of my father's face being superimposed over the face of my new nephew Brian Jeffrey. I got ready for work and just put it in the back of my mind. At work that morning I got an e-mail from my mom. She relayed some news and then she wrote "I was thinking that the baby's eyes look just like Harry's". Harry was my dad. I was floored. It seemed to make sense. I looked at a picture of my nephew and sure enough he has my dad's eyes exactly! Was I

Spring

getting a communication from my dad? Perhaps part of his spirit has reincarnated into baby Brian?

After six months of after-death communications, I am fully convinced that after death we are all very much still connected to each other but that our connection has just changed its form. This is more comforting than any scenario I could have ever wished for. It is more mysterious and more full of hope than any dream.

In my brother's passing I have been given a gift I never would have known to ask for. It is the precise gift I needed. It is a confirmation of all I have felt and suspected to be true my whole life. We are miracles. We are special and we matter. And although the afterlife offers peace, it is imperative that we make the most of our mission here on earth. It is our destiny to keep learning.

4/19/15 I am getting more bold in trying to connect with Duffy in other ways now. Lately I have trying the technique of asking him to show me himself as he is now. I get a visual image of him right away. He is always younger, healthy and usually in some sort of sports attire. Yesterday he was in his surfing wetsuit.

I then make eye contact and ask whatever questions I feel I need to ask. I still feel keenly aware that it is my duty to take care of him. I continue to pray every day that he is in the light, protected, guided and learning.

This morning I had a dream and in it I was telling him that I had spoken to some clients he had worked for. They had said how wonderful he was. I told him this and I saw an image of him smiling and telling me that he was appreciative. He worked hard for so many people who were in pain. He fought insurance companies and worked to give people their lives back. Why couldn't he fight any more for his own life?

4/21/15 I watched my cousin Shari's video of the family tonight. I saw your wedding scene, brother. I could clearly see your expression as you were getting married. During the actual ceremony I was sitting in the back and not able to see you. What struck me was that you had your swagger and I could see the love you felt in the way you held your wife-to-be's hand.

As I watched the video, and saw myself and all of our relatives in their younger incarnations, I have to say "those people are gone." We all exist in an endless stream of moments, aging and changing constantly. We are always becoming something new and always leaving our old selves behind.

4/23/15 Today is the anniversary of my friend's suicide. Another suicide victim in my life! I went online to read the obituaries on Legacy. So many people complimenting his work! He was a deeply caring neurosurgeon. He was honorable and never stooped to performing needless surgeries. It seems he often said no to unwarranted operations and people loved and respected him for this. He was also loved and admired for his gentle, caring, and honest spirit.

I imagine that he too felt deep despair like Duffy. It is unfathomable how such a good man can feel so unworthy. He and Duffy were both good men, both suffering from the disease of depression. I took a moment to pray for my friend and as I was driving home I looked up to see a perfectly round rainbow around the sun. A rainbow with no rain in sight! I know it is a gift from you my friend. I love you and I hope you and Duffy sometimes hang out together!

―――――――――― Spring ――――――――――

4/29/15   Today I left work to go have lunch. When I got into the car, I had a sudden pang of grief and sorrow about Duffy. I was overtaken by the emotion of missing him. As soon as I got on the road Coldplay's *Sky Full of Stars* song came on the radio. It was perfectly timed."

5/7/15   I have been really missing Duffy. I have been praying to the angels and God for his healing and for his peace. I asked that they be with him always and help him to love himself and know he is loved by so many. I prayed about how much I appreciate the contact with him and asked for it to continue. Then I asked him to visit and said "you can show yourself in a stronger way, I won't be afraid."

I put my right hand up and it was very forcefully and very quickly jerked from side to side. It felt like my hand and arm were being electrocuted; a strong bolt of energy moved through them. This was the most intense sensation I have had to date.

5/11/15   My article came out in the Academy of Spirituality and Consciousness Studies Journal a few days ago. I sent a copy to my mom. I called her and we talked. She explained that she was worried because I had been so quiet lately. When we talked about the article, she said she felt that maybe I was not moving forward by asking Duffy to visit every day. She was worried I was stuck. I said this contact made me feel happy and more comfortable in the world.

She told me that sometimes when she is in the garden she almost feels his hands on her shoulders. I said "well that is not really different from what I am experiencing." She said "but you are asking him to come." I told her I felt that when she was in the garden and thinking and remembering him and praying for him she was in her own way inviting him to come to her as well and that there was no difference.

She understood, yet the whole idea that I am asking for him to visit is quite worrisome to her. I am aware that this is quite hard for almost anyone to accept. But it seems so natural to me now.

5/18/15 I have been having very specific images of you, brother, upon waking for several months now. Yesterday I saw you in a lovely red and white shirt. It was very modern. You had on white sunglasses. Again, although I have never seen you in this outfit, it seemed perfectly appropriate to your tastes.

Mom thinks I am possibly intefering with your journey. I want you to know, brother, that if I am doing something wrong, you can stop visiting. I want what is best for you!

It is interesting that even around death we still feel all of the emotions of life—guilt, shame, doubt. I don't think I am hurting anyone and I am enjoying this but what I really want is what is best for Duffy.

5/20/15 I had a strange thing happen last night. When it was time to go to bed, I turned off the light and went to sleep. Sometime later, in the middle of the night, I woke up and the closet light was on! I am sure it was not on when I went to sleep. Sunday is his birthday and so I wonder if he is playing with me!

Then I fell back asleep and dreamt that he was telling me about a book that we both had read a long time ago. I hadn't thought about that book in ages. It's one that talks about the connection between art and physics. We were just talking like we used to, so comfortably.

Spring

I told him that he doesn't have to visit, so I guess if he is coming to me in my dreams, then he is choosing to do so.

5/22/15 It is two days before my brother's birthday. He would have turned fifty one. I miss him so much I can hardly think. Last night I had a very powerful dream. Duffy, me, my dad, and my brother Chris were all in the ocean. The water was unnaturally high. In order to get to the shore I had to carry my clothes at chest level. I was wading through the high waves. Duffy was going quickly ahead of me and Chris was behind me. My brother was being careful; stepping up on the pier carefully. When we got to the water's edge I looked around. There was only a shelf near a door to put my clothes on.

As I laid them down I heard a cat crying. Duffy said we had to put the cat in the closet to keep her from running away. Two little mice came out in dance costumes. As I walked away from the water I turned to the left and opened a door that was suddenly there. I walked into an amazing home. Dad and Duffy followed. As they entered one of them said "I hate it here." I am not sure if it was my dad or Duffy who said this, but I responded strongly to this sentiment.

I looked over the living room and saw the most glorious pool, hot tub, and gardens. The sun was shining on them with a brightness I have never seen. I screamed "Something is wrong with you if you can't appreciate this! Something is wrong!!" I was furious! With that outburst of emotion, both of them quickly jumped into the pool. Before I knew it, both dad and Duffy were smiling and swimming.

When I awoke I felt a sense of sadness as I lay in bed thinking of this. My family has this legacy of depression, negative thinking, and judgement. I used to think that it was the men in my family that embodied this, but I have come to see that I do too. Knowing this, I am more determined than ever to change that legacy!

5/25/15 I had a reading with a medium on Duffy's birthday yesterday. I felt it was the most appropriate way to honor him. A lovely gentleman had contacted me after reading my article in the Academy Journal. He said he was touched by my story and he wanted to offer me a reading for free. He has been doing this for over fifty years. I gratefully accepted! Wow.

I had never done this before. We agreed to have me call him at 1:00 pm. I called at the appointed time and we spoke very briefly before he began. I learned that he has a degree in cultural anthropology and practices art therapy like I do! He explained the parameters and what to expect. He explained to me that a reading is totally unique to the person for whom it is for and that nothing is guaranteed, but to keep my mind open. He also explained that "the spirits decide who wants to come through" and that sometimes it can be quite surprising who does come through. I was ready!

At first a young man stepped forward. He was in his early forties and some type of artist. He had recently passed. I did not immediately recognize who this could be. Then more people came in; my Uncle Herbie, my father and my step father. To my surprise my partner Tom's parents also came. The medium explained that this was not uncommon.

My mother's second husband came in. The medium said he had died of an aneurysm, and indeed he had. At first we thought it was my dad, but it became clear it was my stepfather. He wanted my mother to know that he still loves her and knows she regrets the way she left him. It was a difficult decision for my mom. She loved

Spring

him very much but he had some issues that made it impossible for her to stay with him. I have to admit though that by this time I was wondering, where is my brother?

Eventually, Duffy came in after about half an hour. He was with my dad and my Uncle. My dad referenced calling me by a nickname I had as a child, but he stopped using it as I got older. Duffy too referenced the nickname "T" that he had adopted from our mutual friend. They referred to my "clown" side. This was exciting to me, as I have in my life more than once dressed as a clown for children's events. They also referenced a period in my life—the "fishing around" time—where I was very uncertain about my life.

This was very true. From the age of 24 to 34, I was "fishing around" for what or who I was to be. My dad, my uncle, and Duffy all used to say that I had "landed a big fish" in terms of my finding a career and my path.

I also heard from the medium that a brand new door was about to open for me. I was advised to take it one step at a time and that they would be with me 100%. I have to admit—I found this very exciting—what could this new door be?

I have heard of spirit helpers but never personally felt I had one or knew how to connect with them if I did. It seems a male spirit helper came through in the reading. He spoke of a "blue period" in my life. He said there were still echoes of this for me but that I was going to "come into a joy in life that I never thought possible." This would erase those echoes. It would "be a spiritual door opening inside with changes as well on the outside that would knock my socks off."

Then Duffy spoke. He leaned into the medium and said thank you for doing this. My brother would have done that. He was personable and thoughtful. He said he is very close to me. He said that our relationship goes back a very long time, perhaps many lifetimes. It is a deeply established spiritual relationship. He was sorry that things were cut short. He feels he came here to do what he needed to do and his life had such a richness. He is now astonished reviewing it about how much he did and accomplished. He got so much done in such a short time!

Duffy said he will always be with me. He wanted me to know that he went quickly to the other side. He was greeted by our grandpa. I want to believe he did go quickly; as his death was particularly gruesome to imagine and has kept me wondering many times about how much pain and suffering he may have experienced. He wanted me to know he was happy and I did not need to grieve unnecessarily for him. He said he will be walking through that door with me. What door is this I am wondering?

That was all from Duffy and so it naturally seemed to be the end of the reading. We agreed to stop. We had been at this for over an hour!

After the reading we talked. I learned that as a medium he knew there were ways to access knowledge not fully recognized by society. I reflected on the irony that on this day that I was thinking I would feel so sad, I actually felt blessed to be given this gift by a perfect stranger.

Later that day I shared what I learned with my partner Tom. Surprisingly he was interested. He took it in, and seemed to accept the information and was quite reflective about it. Perhaps this gift touched him as well. I know I will be reflecting on it for quite some time. Tom asked if it gave me comfort and I said that it did. I want to believe that Duffy is fine.

I am realizing more and more as this new communication keeps happening that my "doubting, untrusting, lack of faith" mind is really strong! I feel a sadness about this but at the same time I am

Spring

glad that at least I am aware of it. I also sense that Duffy is giving me the message that I can change this too…one of the key lessons of all this seems to be that anything is possible when I focus on it properly—and when I remember to love myself!!

5/28/15 When I asked for more knowledge this morning, I saw images of Dad, Uncle Herbie and Grand Mom one by one. Are they with you? I hope so! I still pray every day for your healing and peace. I say this for all my loved ones who have passed. May they all be at peace!

I have been dreaming of Duffy a lot since he passed; much more so than I ever dreamt of my father after he died. While lying in bed I got an image of Duffy as a younger man. He said he was in Chile. I said "so I am in Sonoma and you are in Chile and we can communicate?" "Yes" he nodded, "of course!" I told him I have been having a lot of pain lately and asked if there was anything he could do? He leaned over to a cabinet and took out a small rectangular metal box. He mixed up some powdery substance in it and closed the lid. He handed it to me and said to shake it over myself a few times per day. I immediately lifted the invisible box and proceeded to shake the powder over me.

Then a most poignant image came to mind. Duffy and I were outside in a country landscape. It was not familiar, but was very bucolic. I was sitting at the top of a stone wall that he was trying to scale. It was about 7 ft. high. He had on climbing clothes. He got to the top of the wall. He had a look of relief and of peace and I said, "You did it! You got over the wall." He leaned his forehead over to touch mine and we pressed our foreheads against each other for a few seconds. No words were really needed because we both knew what this meant.

Duffy used to describe his depression as a "wall that he had built around himelf that just got higher and higher." He stopped letting us in at the end of his life. Toward the end of his life he just couldn't break through this wall.

I watched as he got down on the other side and started walking with a backpack on his back off toward the horizon. I felt so peaceful and happy for him. I thought that this might mean the end of my feeling his energy on my hands and arms, but as I put my arm out, I felt the strong push of his energy against my right arm and palm. It lasted for about 5 minutes.

6/1/15 This morning I woke up early and said some prayers for you, Duffy and for all of my deceased loved ones. I prayed for your peace and learning and healing. I went back to sleep and had a very vivid dream in which you appeared three times.

In the first part of the dream, we were both sitting at a picnic table outdoors. Behind us was an ancient ruin of some kind. It looked about 40 feet tall, made of stone and covered with vines. I believe there was some kind of pool in front of it. We were talking casually as we use to do when all of a sudden I looked at you and remembered that you were deceased, yet we were talking!

I clearly saw Duffy, smiling, dressed in a casual designer summer shirt. I said "Duffy, I can *see* you!" He smiled. I quickly looked into his eyes and said "I love you so much." We were looking at each other when he began to fade. As his face and shoulders were disappearing, it looked like a hole was forming and a scene of the blue sky with clouds was filling it up. I said "I can't see you now, can you see me?" He said no, but that we should just keep talking. Then after a few seconds he started to come back into view.

Next he and I were at another location and my mother was there. She was younger. I could clearly see Duffy next to me. I said "mom can you see him, Duffy is right here!" She was laughing and said "no." I turned to Duffy and told him to touch her somewhere on her body to see what would happen. He took a small pin and put it in her nose. I then said "did you feel that mom?" She touched her nose and said she could! She started laughing and smiling at this. I told her that was Duffy!

In the third scene, he and I were at an outdoor party of some sort. The landscape was of green trees and lush surroundings, similar to our home in Virginia. My childhood friend Melissa was there. I said to her, "Melissa, I don't want to freak you out, but I can see Duffy, he is right here." He was, too, as clear as before. She did get a little scared and quickly walked off to the side. The dream faded out.

6/4/15 These days my most poignant feelings are of holding two distinctly different realities inside of myself simultaneously. In one reality I am going about my everyday life—and by all outward appearances nothing has changed. But on the inside I am completely different. I now have one ear tuned to this world and another to the world after this world—the river below the river.

My body and my emotional world of grief and loss are real. My body aches, I cry, I long to talk to him and hug him and laugh again, but I know I cannot. On the other hand, the after-death communications I am having have opened my mind up to a new reality that is not physically based, but spiritually based.

This is exhilarating and mysterious and wonderful! The loss and transition has ushered in a new time of tremendous spiritual growth for me. This new reality for me is not either/or; it is "both/and." And I am grateful, too, for now knowing I am far from alone.

6/5/15 I had a vision of Duffy this morning in a beige suit. He was sitting at a bar that was magnificently grand with chandeliers and lots of glass shelves. It looked like it could be in New Orleans. He had his back to me and when I saw him I told him how handsome he looked. His smile made me long for him in this world and I got tearful. I held out my right hand and I told him how much I missed him.

6/15/15 I am here in Myrtle Beach at my cousin's beach house. It is our first family reunion since Duffy's death. It is so bittersweet for us all to be together without Duffy. My cousin has generously let us stay for a whole week. It is heavenly. Last night I saw some old friends who drove me from the airport in Charlotte to the beach house in South Carolina. They hadn't seen me since before my brother passed. Of course they wanted to know how I was doing.

    I shared my thoughts and feelings with them. Remarkably one of my friends more than understood and had words of comfort that helped my heart mend. She shared a personal story with me.

    At one time she was married to a very dangerous man. She said that in the beginning he was not that way. He was charming and captivating and seemed to have a laser-like focus on her that she accepted as normal, even flattering.

    Over time this focus became an obsession and a desire to control her at any cost. He increasingly became more jealous, controlling and violent. She was too scared to leave but knew she had to in order to survive. By the time she discovered evidence of his affairs she was ready to flee. Finally, in the middle of the night, she found her chance to flee. She was on another continent and so getting away from him would not be easy. That night while he

Spring

was out, she drove to the airport and got herself on a plane back to the States.

By this time she was emotionally and psychologically shattered. She had dismissed his lies and cruelty as anomalies. He always had good reasons for his anger. He told her the affairs were all in her head.

She told me the realization that her husband's true character was not the nice interesting man she initially fell for, but this violent, manipulative person flung her into a state of panic. Everything she thought to be true about the world was turned upside down. Her sense of self, her ability to know the truth and trust her own senses and judgment was gone. Once home, she isolated herself from everyone in order to heal. It took her nine months of solitude to come to terms with her nightmare.

She said that perhaps Duffy had a hole so big inside of himself that he could never fill it. Maybe he had lost all faith in himself.

Summer

6/23/15 I've been back East for our family reunion in Myrtle Beach for a few days now. We have bonded and laughed. We each hold Duffy in our hearts every minute. Our love is palpable for our missing piece of the family. I once heard that you can never replace the person at the table, but you can keep a table setting in your heart and mind for them. I think we have all been feeling that this week. We are a strong family; determined to look forward. We all know he would want that; so we carry on and enjoy each other as much as possible. Now that we have three new babies in the family there is new life and new hope for us.

After my family's time together. I made my way down the coast toward Savannah.

I was going right past Charleston and was not planning on stopping. As I was driving over the bridge near the first exit I had the thought, "God, take me around today to do what you wish for me."

Just then I found myself taking the exit into downtown Charleston. I found a place to park and got out of my car to suffocating heat. I started walking down the main street and I quickly realized I was on the street where earlier in the week nine church members had been gunned down by one of their own. As I walked I saw people with flowers. Men were handing out water, women were praying, little girls were dressed in their Sunday best. As I approached I realized I had come upon the very church where earlier in the week this awful tragedy had occurred.

As I stood in front of the church all I could see was a wall of flowers. People were bringing more in a steady stream to place at the church walls. I looked up to see the tall, white spires of Emanuel AME church. I have never seen such a church!

The walls were bright white, in contrast to the blue sky. The spires rose up impossibly tall and seemed to pierce the clouds. The feeling all around was indescribable.

Children placed flowers, their mothers guiding them. Everyone was smiling, polite, reverent and calm. It was the most peaceful and most other-worldly feeling I have ever had. It felt as if the veil between life and death had been lifted. I felt the souls of those who had passed still there, witnessing the love and the peace of the scene.

I talked to people the rest of the day about this. They all told me a similar thing, which was, in the wake of the shooting Charleston decided "We will meet ultimate evil with ultimate forgiveness."

I took a town trolley around to see the rest of Charleston. I got on and was ushered to the back of the bus. I sat next to an old African American man. I couldn't help but think how not too long ago our friends were given the back of the bus as their only option.

The man next to me on the trolley looked at the scene at the church as we drove by. His eyes looked sad and weary. I smiled and said, "It's sad, yet people are so kind." He nodded and remarked that it was indeed so.

I could not believe the kindness, the maturity, and the grace that was being exhibited all around me. It was as if everyone in the town got an invisible memo: "meet this day with the kindness and peace we know is possible."

Summer

I feel so amazingly privileged to have been here. It seems the whole city had its heart open today. The power of this was unmistakable: the pure feeling of safety, comfort and connection.

Later in the day I was shopping and walked into a local boutique in a beautiful coastal town just south of Charleston.

I started talking to the shopkeeper about my experience at the church today. She was so open. I mentioned my brother had passed last summer and she shared about her experience involving her father's passing. She told me that as he was ailing, she knew she had to get to the hospital to see him as he was very close to the end. Her other family members did not feel the urgency but somehow she did. She choose to listen to her gut and closed the shop and started driving to be with him.

As she was driving to the hospital, she looked up to see the sunset colors over the horizon. And then, filling the sky, she saw an angel lit from behind by the sun. She watched as this apparition glided across the sky.

She was so matter of fact about it. She believed it was a sign that her father would be guided from this world in loving care by God. I was curious about her matter-of-fact acceptance of seeing the angel.

I asked if she really saw it or if it was more like the clouds made the shape of an angel? "No," she said it was definitely an angel—not clouds—and she was very comfortable with her knowledge of being given that gift. She said that a few days later she went into a thrift store. There she spied a small terra cotta planter in the shape of an angel. She said it looked so much like the angel she saw in the sky that she had to get it.

We talked about how these experiences of synchronicity are comforting. She believes in God and feels that she was being reassured that all is well. I told her that I did not know what it all meant. I agreed with her that it was comforting and that maybe what is most important is that some force in the universe cares about our comfort! I felt reassured by our discussion. It gave me more fuel to continue to write about my ongoing connection with Duffy.

7/5/15 July is turning out to be a very rough month for me emotionally. Yesterday on the Fourth I thought about the fact that it was your wedding anniversary. I remember the numbing sadness in you just one year ago. It is so painful to think about. I held my hand up and asked to hold yours and to feel you on my hand. I felt a strong stroke on my fingers and then my hand was moved sideways.

I prayed that you would understand that even though our family is struggling we are moving forward. We do not feel anger at you or judgment. We understand that you could not stay in so much pain.

7/6/15 As I was driving to work this morning a song we used to love *Don't Dream It's Over* by Crowded House came on the radio. As it was playing I looked up to see the license plate in front of me: "DFF". Hi Duff! The song has even more meaning for me because it talks about the walls between people. Duffy felt he had built so many walls by the end of his life that he could not find a way over them. He was imprisoned behind those self-made walls. But the song says, "…they come to build a wall between us, you know they won't win…" I think Duffy is saying "Fear won't win—love will."

As the anniversary date of Duffy's death approaches I find myself crying a lot—out of the blue—and fiercely. The ripples of grief go through my body and my blood feels like it is boiling over with loss. I am reminded of other losses and some days the grief is compounded. I know my brother Chris and my mom are both struggling now too. We each have our own ways of dealing with the grief. I am

Summer

continuing to write about the other side of this journey-which is my on-going connection with his spirit.

7/14/15 The past few days I have meditated on the Tibetan Buddhist deity, Green Tara. I have asked her spirit to join mine and make me stronger. Tara is a heart-centered deity. She seems to embody a dynamic equilibrium; not dispassionate or disconnected, but wholly engaged. Her eyes almost look crossed as if to signify she is focused on the inner world. She is non-judgmental and allowing. She is movement and stillness in action at once. I prayed to her for help, healing, and wisdom. I prayed not just for general healing but for a deep cleansing of all the significant grief in me. Last night I had a powerful encounter that I think Tara helped with. I was asking Duffy to visit, but instead I got a very strong sense of an old lover!

He was a handsome, intelligent man with a deep wounding at a young age. He and I had near perfect communication where we did not have to say anything to understand each other. We had a brief relationship, nothing long lasting. He ended up going to medical school and marrying the woman of his dreams. He always used to ask me if I was happy. I would ask him as well. Tragically, a few years ago I discovered that he had passed away by committing suicide. So much talent, love and kindness- gone.

His spirit became present to me as I lay in bed. I got images of our past relationship, things we did together like jogging and going to the beach. I felt my body get lighter and then I had a sense that his spirit seemed to be floating over me. It seemed as though my former lover's spirit and mine had joined. I felt comforted and supremely loved.

I received the image of he and I walking together one night and he picking a rose and handing it to me. I saw his wedding day and I remembered that Duffy drove me there and we attended it together. I then had the realization that for much of my life I felt as though I was the "not good enough girl." Certainly in this case, my ex chose the slim blond over me. At the wedding I felt so awkward, ugly—a cast off—and yet I attended because I felt it was the right thing to do.

In the merging of our spirits and the images shown to me, I feel he was telling me that my feelings of inferiority were no longer necessary, and no longer served me. It was a powerful moment. I felt his spirit lift away and I thanked him for what he gave to me—the knowledge that I am fine as I am.

7/15/15 Last night I was asking Duffy to visit me when I went to bed. I was asking him why he died so early, and why he suffered so. To my surprise I got a vision of my father. He was stepping in, I felt, to take some of the responsibility for my brother's passing. His face was showing me "It is my doing."

I got images of my father and Duffy as a child, playing ball together, talking. It seemed as though my father was showing me that he is now taking care of my brother in a way in which he could not when my brother went to live with him after my parents divorced.

Duffy was always honest and open with me about the fact that he felt that he was on his own and that our father had neglected him. He even asserted that he never got to be a kid and he wasn't really taught wrong from right. He only had the guidance of our mother a few weeks out of the year. And he only got to see Chris and I on holidays and during the summers.

I also saw images of my father and myself together when I was young. I saw and felt and sensed things I had forgotten about; there were the stuffed animals my father gave me, the sharing of all kinds of wonderful foods together, the taste of his coffee in the morning, my Christmas party dress when I was 5 yrs. old.

I felt all that my father did for me. I asked him, "Why did you leave so soon?" I received the thought that he would have dragged me down if he had lived and that he is better able to guide me from the other side. I asked him "But what about all of the things we never got to experience together?" His response was that it would not have been like that, he was not well and he would have been unable to do anything but emotionally exhaust me.

7/19/15   I said good morning to Duffy and asked for some contact. I saw images of mean dogs, blades, scary things. I asked him why he was showing me these scary things? Then I saw a large amount of marijuana. Duffy had an addiction to it as well as to other substances. It seems he was showing me how his addiction had him imprisoned. He seemed possessed. I asked if I could help him. I then saw something like black tar around his heart. I pulled it all out. I said a prayer that the wisdom of Green Tara would fill him. I blessed his third eye and finally, told the inhabiting destructive spirits to leave.

I saw them fly out of him toward a faraway landscape. He was sweating so I wrapped a blanket around him. I saw a bed covered in banana leaves and helped him lie down. I said, "Rest dear brother and awaken to a new you." A few minutes passed and then I saw a faint, white outline of Duffy rise up from his body. It left his old body lying on the table like a wetsuit. He became shapes and colors which were swirling around me. He said he felt so much lighter. He changed form again into a silver disc, expanding over great distances and then contracting. I saw a big Duffy smile, and tear-filled eyes. He was happy. I told him I hoped I had helped him because I love him so!

Chapter 8

Anniversary

7/23/15 This morning an image of Duffy came into my mind. I feel he was showing me something very important on this, the eve of the anniversary of his passing. I saw him sitting on a park bench with his hands tied behind his back. The scene was light and calm. He was looking straight ahead with a passive, peaceful look on his face. It alarmed me at first. I was scared that he was showing me he was in pain.

But then I saw him lie down on his back on the bench. His hands were now free and the rope was lying on his chest. He turned his head to the side and went to sleep. He was at peace. Then a whole flock of white birds came flying out from his body. They rose up in the air in front of me. The scene was light and calm.

Duffy was shedding his body—the form I had identified as "him." He is now in full spirit and the white birds are a symbol of that spirit. He wants me to know that he is no longer in bondage, symbolized by the ropes holding his hands together. He is now in a new and freer form.

Never Parted

It has been a very tough week. My body has cried till it hurt and I have had many loved ones say the kindest things. My family is feeling the hole in our life, the space Duffy used to occupy. I know I am not out of the woods from being fine one day and emotionally wrought the next, but I am moving closer to more understanding.

Today I feel a bit of fresh air, a bit of belief that I can once again feel the magic in life and fully feel joy once more. I can have adventures and not feel guilty. I am wanting to move on, and am determined to live life in a manner my brother would be happy about.

I know that I must continue to live my life as openly as possible, with the willingness to learn as much as I can about that which is so hard to explain! Duffy would be all for it and I do believe he has a hand in it.

7/25/15 I made it through the anniversary of Duffy's passing with love and support from my friends and family. Everyone was so kind. In a way the actual day itself was easier than the days leading up to it, which were full of anxiousness and sadness in missing him.

But on the evening of July 24th a most remarkable thing happened! I did my usual relaxation and meditation to say hi to Duffy. Because I was especially sensitive I asked if he would show up in another form, other than the energy I have been feeling on my hands. In retrospect, I was still acting "needy." Well, what I got in response was the song by the Guess Who *No Time (left for you)*! At first I was quite taken aback. But then I realized that this must have been sent from Duffy because I barely even know the song and the timing of it showing up when I was asking for more is telling. The words were profound in Duffy's message to me.... "on my way to better things, going to grow some wings..distant roads are calling me. Seasons change and so did I, you need not wonder why..."

Anniversary

The message for me was unmistakable. In my attachment to his old form, my being caught in the net of time, I have to let go and realize he is out of time. Duffy spoke clearly through a song coming into my mind. I got the message! What is most important is that he is ok.

It seems that now may be the perfect time to let go of his old form and embrace my new relationship to him. I now know I can connect to him through stillness and deep listening. He must sense that I am ready.

7/26/15 This morning I got an image of the Torrey Pines Glider Park as I awoke. I could smell the salt air and see the hangliders. I saw Duffy sitting on the grass. In going with "this new normal," I participated in the scene. I sat down next to him and we talked to each other like we used to. I asked how he was and he said "good." He asked how I was and I began to get tearful. "It's obvious I am just above the water line. I miss you like crazy. So, you know, just trying to move forward with some dignity." He took my hand and we held hands silently looking out to sea.

After a few minutes he said "let's walk". We walked over to where his funeral was held. I asked if he was present at it and knew we were all there. He said yes, he did. Suddenly I was overcome as the feelings of the loss of my brother descended once again on me. I wanted to stay with him but it was just too painful for me. I guess I hadn't fully embraced the reality of our new connection. We got into his Porsche. I said, "you know, part of me just wants to drive anywhere with you and the other part of me wants to go back to my bed and be back in my current life."

And so I said "until next time," and felt myself snuggled back between the covers in my own bed. I allowed myself to feel that

Never Parted

I was able to be in two places at once; part of me with Duffy and part of me here in my present life. It was a comforting solution to wanting to be with him.

*No one knows
the reason for any of this —
why even make it a question?*

Death doesn't.

*The unleashed wonder
of that moment is sufficient
to still any speculation.*

*This is not a metaphor —
it will be the same door opening
inward that once opened out.*

*I am that swinging door,
not knowing in from out,
death from life, me from you.*

What is surrender?
—Bob O'Hearn

7/31/15 I had a beautiful visitation from Duffy last night. I saw Duffy clear as a bell, dressed in a beautiful lavender shirt. He had on nice, casual pants and he was in radiant health. He looked to be in his thirties, with thick curly hair. He was smiling, relaxed and poised.

Anniversary

8/5/15 This morning I decided to try having a conversation with Duffy using a technique where I imagine us together in a peaceful place. I got quiet and still and relaxed and imagined myself sitting on the bench outside of his condominium on the water. I asked if he would like to visit me. I saw him come toward me through the gate to the sitting area.

He had on a casual short sleeve shirt with stripes. He stood next to the bench. I said "Hey—I am so glad to see you!" He smiled and looked at me and then out at the horizon.

He sat down next to me. We started talking just like we used to. What was striking was the way in which he responded; he talked and looked at me exactly like he always did. I asked him if he was happy and about what he was doing now. He went into a description of how he is involved in moving "planes of existence." I asked what that meant. He said it was kind of like architecture and building and physics. I asked if he was designing too and he said it all went together.

He went on to explain that the planes of existence are of geometric shapes and huge in size. He said he was also working with lights. I asked if he was working with people the way he used to and he smirked the Duffy smirk. He responded that he was working with teams to move these planes, but that he was not directly working with people and it was a relief. He always loved building things and architecture in general, as I reminded him. I told him I was happy to hear that he was using his mind in a way he loved.

I asked if he had a relationship. He smiled and looked to the side, tilting his head. He told me that here, he had many relationships that were deeply heartfelt and connected. But, that it was not like it is here on earth. There is not the distinction of ok, I am with this person now in this way and not that person. He said relationships were more flowing, connected, always happening, and part of existence as much as anything.

I asked if I was causing him harm by asking him to reach out to me when I hold my hands out. I could tell he was reluctant to say yes and instead he said, "in a way." I asked if we could compromise and if I could ask just once a week from now on. He agreed that this would be fine and doable for him. It would not interfere with him doing his work now.

I also asked if we could play a game. I wanted to ask for some things to show up in my physical world as a sign he was communicating with me. He said ok, we could do this.

I asked for some green glass and an unusually colored butterfly. He smiled. He then took my hand and we sat holding hands. I put my head on his shoulder and cried. We got up from the bench together and walked to the gate.

I asked him to go first and I said I was fine because I was with him, even as I was lying in bed and simultaneously looking at the water. I asked if I could do anything for him. He thought for a second and then looked at me and let me know what he needed was for me to look into his eyes. We looked at each other for about a minute. I could see into his soul in that moment.

I watched him walk away from me. He walked toward the lookout platform on the edge of the cliff; a favorite place of his. I looked out at the water and then brought my awareness back to my room. I wanted to be the first to leave the scene.

What joy, what peace, what a great meeting. He was so present. We conversed like we used to! Tomorrow I will be faithfully looking for the glass and the butterfly!

Anniversary

8/7/15 I'm so excited to say that my virtual reality experiment was a success yesterday. I had asked Duffy if we could play a game. I asked him to make two items appear, some green glass and an unusually colored butterfly. The butterfly came to mind first followed by the glass. I choose the glass because I had remembered a green drinking glass he had in his house. It was a sort of lime green and he loved the color green.

Well I was going to work and I got out of my car on the way to get coffee, I did a quick stretch and when my eyes looked down at the ground there by my foot was a tiny piece of green glass, a tiny broken piece shining in the sun. I couldn't believe it. I scooped it up and got in my car.

I forgot about the butterfly request once I got to work. We had a staff meeting early and I scrambled to get there. I sat down by my co-worker and we began. She said something to me and as I looked at her I saw on her ear was a small, purple earring in the shape of a butterfly! I think my mouth dropped open. Not only did Duffy answer my request, but he did it so quickly!

8/8/15 I talked to a new friend this morning about my new understanding of reality since Duffy died. He was very open and curious. We talked about why is life (and death) the way it is? We came up with the possibility that we are born here to become more and more adept at being free from fear. But there are so many questions—what is fear, really? And what of the dead—are they truly free?

Perhaps through each connection with the deceased we as a species move one step closer to being free from the illusion of fear. Maybe we will someday live knowing we go on forever.

Never Parted

8/15/15 Yesterday I imagined Duffy and I together on a surfboard in the ocean. He was tugging at his bathing suit, trying to pull it up higher. I teased him as usual, like I had through our whole lives. "Maybe you've lost some pounds." He smirked, a half smile, full of meaning in response. We always made jokes about our fluctuating weight. It was a common source of amusement for us was when we were around our mother, who usually pointed out whenever one of us had fallen off the wagon and gained some poundage.

I launched into questions. How are you? He looked relaxed around the eyes, "Ok." Duffy had a way of talking where one felt like part of his mind was with you, considering the conversation with great attention and the other part of his mind was working out the great questions of life. I wanted to ask him all kinds of questions, but restrained myself.

I did ask about his happiness. Are you happy brother? His eyes were gazing far off. He seemed to be feeling so much. I'm not sure what he was feeling, and it pained me to not know, to not be able to share his innermost thoughts.

I asked if he could change his age; slip into another role? Yes, he could! He then turned into a toddler before my eyes and bounced on the surfboard.

He changed back and explained that he could become any age, any role from many lifetimes. It was all a certain level of vibration that he just had to slip into. He showed me a visual. I saw him lean forward and behind him was a wave of bodies, in all sizes and shapes. He said it was easy but of course he was new to it. He said he could even be the old man he never got to be in this lifetime.

I became aware of it being time to say goodbye. I asked if he would leave first. He said "ok," and swam out from the board. He looked back, ducked under the water and then all I could see was a fast-moving ripple of water. Duffy was moving rocket fast away from me.

Autumn... Again

11/01/15 I've been sorting out my thoughts and impressions from the ASCS (Academy for Spirituality and Consciousness Studies) conference on after-death communication in September. I met so many brave and open-hearted people there. Some had lost their children to freaky things like snowboarding accidents. How do you grieve the loss of a twenty year old boy? So full of life and then suddenly cut short? The women and men I met had clear and firm beliefs in the afterlife communications they had been getting from their loved ones. Many had never considered the possibility of such a thing but came to accept and believe it after their losses and subsequent experiences.

Some of the people at the conference, I could tell, were on the edge of accepting what they were experiencing. They had their reasons for doubt, yet the power of their own curiosity and their need to know more got them to the conference.

The presenters were diverse and intriguing. Some were the real deal—genuine and amazing in what they had personally experienced—and what they could convey about life after death. Other presenters were more disappointing. And some were downright awe inspiring.

One such person was a mother who had lost her teenage son. She was a Midwestern wife and mother whom she self-described as not particularly spiritual and not a believer in the afterlife—before

Never Parted

her son passed. After his death, she began having many synchronicities—amusingly in the form of songs her son would send her. It took a while for her to get used to this and to process her grief. When she got strong enough she decided to try and have a more concrete way of communicating with him. So, she began using a pendulum and an alpha numeric board. She has been doing this for many years. Now in workshops she teaches others the techniques she has perfected.

11/3/15 Today I begin my trip to San Diego to see my nephew turn one. We have had such a tough year and yet here is this little one shining so brightly every day. In driving from Sonoma to Big Sur today it was raining. Big shafts of glorious bright light shone through the sky onto the ocean as I drove down Hwy 1. The water is an unreal turquoise blue and the sky silver and stormy. Duffy's friends took some of his ashes and buried them here, in a creek in Big Sur. I feel the power of the place and the power of my love for my brother as I drive along the coast.

I got to my favorite spot, the Nepenthe cafe in Bug Sur. There were only two cars in the parking lot. To my delight, one of the cars was an exact double of Duffy's dark blue Porsche! What was even better was the license plate said "Hef." This was a nickname from some of his dear friends in San Diego. Too cool. I feel so loved.

As I was driving away I rounded the bend. People were out of their cars, standing in the rain, looking up and taking pictures. I looked up and saw a full rainbow over the hill. A shaft of light shone on the highest rock, making it look brightly golden. The Beach Boys *Good Vibrations* was playing, only to be followed by a fantastic line up of tunes. Ziggy Marley, The Who—*Love Reign o'er Me*. And of course Bruce Springsteen's *Tenth Avenue Freeze Out.*

Autumn…Again

Duffy, you out-did yourself! The light on the water and on the aloe covered hills was ethereal. I'll never forget how beautiful the scene was. Exactly like your spirit!

In the following days I got a phone message from one of Duffy's dear friends. She had lived with him briefly after his divorce. She cared deeply for my brother, as so many did. She let me know that when she showed up last week at the airport for her flying lesson she was greeted by a new pilot. He introduced himself as Duffy. She found out this week that his given name is Jeff! She can't wait until the next time I come to visit and Duffy takes us flying.

I can't wait, either!

Chapter 9

Virtues

I decided to ask Duffy what he would like to share with others from his new perspective. I prayed and asked that he show me what he wants me to share. I got the answer *clearly*. He wants me to share some of the virtues that he lived his life by.

The first virtue is "Excellence." I meditated on the virtue of excellence and I wrote down what came to mind, from Duffy, through automatic writing.

What follows are the most important virtues to Duffy, as communicated by him to me. They are meant to help us here on earth live our lives to the fullest and to learn from the perspective of a soul who is now seeing from a larger, more loving perspective.

Excellence

I have strived my whole life for excellence. Whether it was in my athletics—rowing crew, doing marathons, biking, skiing— or my work and career, my relationships, caring for my family.

Never Parted

I always had an eye for asking "how can this be better?" Many times I know it left me feeling unsatisfied in the moment. From here I can see that it didn't have to be either/or. I could have asked and analyzed how it could be better and yet still appreciate the moment. I pushed myself constantly. It was a way of life for me. I had to have my whole heart and mind in something or I could not do it. I know from the outside I appeared to be so laissez-faire and able to let the little things go but on the inside my mind was always working, wondering, and asking.

What I did not realize I needed to do was to take the concept of excellence to my own personal inner development. I was my father's son. So much of what I did, I did for external rewards. I told myself it was for my own personal best, but what I came to realize at the end of my life is that my own personal best somehow got replaced by always trying to conform to others' expectations. I became excellent at being a chameleon. This did not happen overnight. It was insidious and ultimately expedited my rise in income and status.

I was like two people in one. I had the part of me that craved the simple things and was pleased by them. The other part desired more and better things. This produced great stress in me. I did not realize the stress until things went wrong. The first time my business was really threatened I could not cope. I could not accept the idea of failure. My perspective had become so warped—I believed that my identity was defined by what I could do and give to others. If that ended then I was a total failure.

From here I can see that excellence means something else. It means never compromising your own true self for others. Live in the glory of your own passions, interests, and desires. Make the most of your own true strengths and build up skills that you find pleasure in. To live in excellence is to live as yourself as much as you can.

Don't be swayed by the pressures of others' expectations. Follow your heart and your energy will flow too. The combination will be true excellence. But the heart part has to come first!

Determination

Determination means not giving in, even when you hurt. Even if you fear failure never say or think you can't do what you set your mind to. Determination is a way of life. It is strength to do what you must when others are counting on you. In my life I was much more determined when I set a goal to reach for myself. Never accepting what is, but, going further. I was determined to succeed, to provide for my family. Often I didn't feel well, battling depression or anxiety. But, I kept at my work for my family. It gave me a purpose. Knowing people depended on me kept me going despite my own resistance. I realize from here, that my own personal pleasure did not drive much of my determination, although it may have looked that way to others. A sense of responsibility to others channeled my will.

I have no regrets. I loved my wife and family and I never imagined I would give up at the end; but I did.

I don't want anyone to feel sad for me. I lived my life to the fullest. Many times to excess. I did what I wanted much of the time. I played and worked and loved hard. I realize now I gambled with my life in using drugs and I undermined my own determination with this gambling attitude. I didn't realize that I really did have a serious problem with drugs. I was searching for something I now see that I could not seem to find in my life, despite all I had. In a big part I was searching for peace and relief from debilitating bouts of depression and anxiety. I thought I could party it away.

Although it seems I lost the big gamble and lost my life, I say from here, NO! I took my life in order to go on as I desire. I wanted to be free; I was determined when I chose to take my own life. I know this may be hard for some to hear, but I chose to die with all of the determination I had.

I see from here, that determination to live in the most joyous way possible is what is important. To do whatever it takes to make your life all it can be by surrounding yourself with people who love you, making good choices for yourself, putting yourself and others on equal footing and marching to the beat of your own drummer is what it is about.

Kindness

If I had to choose the most important virtue, it would be kindness. Without it, life is hollow. So often we forget to be kind. Unknowingly we hurt others' feelings in the blink of an eye. What cannot be undone is the harm we do to our relationships. I did not realize until it was too late that my moments of anger left a mark on some of my relationships.

So many times I came out of the vicious cycle of depression and hypomania to find the aftermath of the tornado I created. I wish I had been able to see what was happening while I was in it. But, the reality of having a mental illness is that often you cannot see what is happening until afterward, if ever.

I know I was often kind, maybe too kind, to some who would take advantage. But I would not change that.

From here it is clear that our number one job on earth is to be kind. To always extend a hand and to not withhold love.

Most importantly be kind to yourself, be gentle with your own failings. Don't judge yourself—rather keep acknowledging how far you have come. There is no failure in earthly life. It is false. Focus on extending joy and kindness as you go along your journey.

Charity

For me this is the meaning of life. To be charitable is to be the best human you can be. We are nothing without our love and caring for each other. Who are we to judge?

Who will be next in needing a helping hand? If we can we should extend our hands to others in order to help. It takes nothing from us and connects us all the more. Make life easier and be willing to do what you can for others. Your charity will be a reward in itself.

I tried to help my friends and family whenever I could, just because I cared for them. I never thought about what I might have to sacrifice or lose. I just did it naturally.

I can see now that this was a strength and a way in which I was in touch with what was important. We are not judged in the afterlife. We are guided to learn from our actions. No harsh punishment awaits us, only more knowledge and love.

We should be developing a more giving heart on the earthly plane. To be charitable is to generate love. To be charitable is to give others room for their imperfections; to not judge them for their mistakes. A charitable attitude brings forth compassion when we live from a place of acceptance and not judgment of others.

I was not able to be as accepting of my own mistakes—to be so charitable to myself. I paid the price for this with my sense of failure and shame.

Hope

I lived my life like a bird flying toward some great horizon. I was alive with energy to spare. I flew forward—daringly and recklessly. I spoke about hope to my friends, but there were times in my life that I was hard pressed to find it for myself.

Hope is our birthright. It makes us alive with energy. It gives us peace and soothes us when all else fails. Hope is the fuel of God. We are not just atoms, flesh, and bone; we are the movement of divine light. What matters in being human is to be there for each other: to hope, to care.

I put up walls between myself and those who tried to offer me hope. And behind those walls I died.

Here I am free. Together with others who are just one world away from yours.

We want to share!

We want to give hope!

We live!

You are loved!

Reach out your hands—and take hold of it!

Chapter 10

Nothing to Fear

I just read a most interesting book called "Why Science is Wrong" by Alex Tsakiris. In it he argues against the current scientific stance that says that consciousness is meaningless. He says that "You are not meaningless; your conscious experience isn't meaningless. And the feelings you have for the most important people in your life are not meaningless." At the end of the book he advises "Follow the data, wherever it leads."

It seems I have been leading my own private science experiment. It is a sort of one woman experiment. I haven't really been thinking about it in this way but here it is: I have been having experiences, recording them and repeating them. The interpretation, of course, is mine alone. What is helpful is that I know now from reading many books about after-death communications that my experiences are hardly different from so many others in similar situations.

The following are some of the teachings I have received from Duffy obtained through the technique of automatic writing, that have to do with the nature of his reality now, our reality on earth and the afterlife.

NOTE: The comments below are graciously provided by A.B. Scott-Hill B.E. (Elect.) who wrote the 2016 science book, *"The Paranormal is Normal" (The Science Validation to Reincarnation, the Paranormal and your Immortality).*

Regarding the format chosen below, comments are shown in italics and the references shown within the comments refer to the References page—which gives some references applicable detail. Underlining of words in Duffy's responses is used to denote those words which specifically apply to the immediately following comments. Where new information is thought to be given by Duffy, this is highlighted by stating "new information" with inverted commas—to suggest this.

Question No 1

Terri: What form do you take now?

Duffy: Terri, I am in all forms; yes, electricity, molecules, cellular, sun, wind, sky…get it?

Comments: *This conforms to the principle that when a discarnate; one basically has a photon characteristic and can appear as light e.g., an orb. But there is strong independent scientific evidence that we have the option in the afterlife to appear as almost anything—simply by thought and as inferred above by Duffy. (Ref: 1)*

Duffy Cont.: No, well let me see if I can explain. I exist—yes, I do! But not how you think of me—no more Duffy curls, smile, sense of humor—those things are not me now. Me is everywhere. All at once. Yes, I am still "me" and always will be. You too, will always be you. However, we lose our "one" self and become part of the many-selves. I'm a part and I am whole. Not diminished at all. I am grander in a way, really, that is hard to explain.

Comment Cont. There are two important concepts here—the first is that after "transition", one becomes aware of the fact that—as covered in detail in Jane Robert's channeled "Seth" books and elsewhere—that we are all part of a "super-self" (Ref 2:), which has a number of selves who like ourselves can experience many earth lives, simultaneously. The other underlying and important concept reflected by Duffy is: "Me is everywhere. All at once." *and later,* "I'm a part and am whole", *which aligns with the Biblical concept That we are all one, with each other and with God. And on earth, we suffer the illusion/distortion in thinking that we are separate. This may well be the most fundamental concept in the multiverse and is Duffy's first teaching. (Ref: 3) In just those few words of Duffy,* "Me is everywhere" *indicates Duffy's existence in non-physical reality, where quantum physics is prime and where time does not exist and space is irrelevant. A discarnate entity can travel anywhere in space instantly if desired. (Ref: 4) Not entirely "new information" but provides a strong validation for Terri's mediumship. It also provides useful teaching by Duffy.*

Question No 2

Terri: Can you hear my thoughts?

Duffy: I can hear your thoughts because the connection of everything in the universe is thought. Actually, I am closer than a thought. I feel your intent to think of me—I already know it. We know intent and thoughts just "are."

Comments: All objects in the Universe at a quantum level are entangled (interconnected) holistically with one another, so that a discarnate and thoughts (thoughts are also "things" and quantum) can associate instantly with anything else via the zero-point field (which intermingles with everything in the universe). There are many references to support what Duffy says here, and with considerable science *support. There is even a book which largely focusses on the Zero-point field. Also, the concepts of intent and attention are important facets of replicated laboratory research findings which have been shown to increase telepathic results. The concept of a discarnate being able to even "feel your intent to think of me"—as Duffy said, illustrates the amazing power of thought available to a discarnate, suggested by the famous maxim that "faith can move mountains." But the concept of the importance of "intent" and power of thought is also highlighted in other channeled literature. Duffy's comments here are therefore both illuminating and validating for Terri. (Ref: 5)*

Question No 3

Terri: Do you have friends?

Duffy: <u>Well we have groups</u>, rather than friends. <u>Groups of like or equal minded souls</u>. <u>We have a purpose together—to create, grow, learn and expand</u>. I'm part of more than one group. They blend together to make me whole always in a synergistic way unique to me and to my needs for growth.

Comments: The "groups" mentioned here are well supported by Dr. Michael Newton's books (where multiple instances of life-between-life professional hypnotic regressions are used). He calls them "cluster groups" and outlines their activities in detail. (Ref: 6) The second portion of this teaching appears to be "new information," as I have not read it anywhere else. I did not know one participates in more than one cluster group or that "each group blends" to help each other's needs for growth. Thus, this seems to be "new information" and assists our knowledge and validation.

Question No 4

Terri: Do you ever get bored?

Duffy: No, no boredom! Only constant potential.

Comment: *Good to know for certain one never gets bored. There is a reference that there is some expectation of this.* "New information" (Ref:7)

Question No 7

Terri: Does prayer matter? Does it change anything?

Duffy: Prayer does matter—it shows intent. Intent matters and is what changes things. It changes the direction of energy.

Comments: *This aligns with Question 2 comments and references but goes a little further. As said previously, there is good scientific evidence to support the effectiveness of prayer and intent. The sentence* "It changes the <u>direction</u> of energy", *though, could be new information.* (Ref: Same as Q2)

Question No 8

Terri: Will we be together again?

Duffy: Yes, we will! I promise! <u>We are all partly here on Earth or in other incarnations and partly home.</u> (Ref: Same as Q1 Ref2) I will come back to Earth to learn the lessons I did not get.

Comment: *A common reincarnational comment, but covered copiously in literature. Nevertheless validating.*

Question No 9

Terri: Any advice for me?

Duffy: Please don't try and be there for so many who may not believe what you are sharing. Just try and find a way out to the edges of life and belief—inside of yourself. Be you first, then maybe be there for others! Do the projects, but BE YOU! Get it? Be careful you don't waste precious time on false idols. They will suck you dry. Instead, plan carefully where and who and why you engage. Your spirit is sparkly and delicate and special. Don't waste it. What you do is different from who you are. Don't forget that. What you do should serve <u>who</u> you are. <u>Much of the illusion of life on Earth is of the importance of "activities." But, they are not real in a sense. What is real is the spirit energy, life propelled on with the fuel of soul intent. Be intent on wise action! Everything reflects the true intentions of our souls.</u>

<u>Comments:</u> *This is "new information" and useful in the concept that the critical issue is not everyday life but, as Duffy says; "<u>Everything reflects the true intentions of our souls.</u>" The word "illusions" is in itself validating—as it is classically used by discarnates to convey differences from their realm—often seen in "dualities" such as love/hatred ("hatred" is an Earth experience only), good/evil (evil is an Earth experience only) etc. (No Ref.)*

Question No 10

Terri: What would you like to show me today?

Duffy is standing holding a book.

Duffy: It is the book of knowledge. It's all in there. They give them out here.

<u>Comments:</u> *"New Information". I have never heard of this before, but it sounds <u>eminently logical</u>—as <u>many</u> incarnations on earth, and copious teachings received as discarnates, suggests there is a mountain of knowledge/information to learn. (No Ref.)*

Question No 11

Terri: What happens when we die? What happens when we first pass over?

Duffy: When a person dies and first passes over, <u>it feels like being in the shower. It is <u>warm all around, there is some rhythmic sound</u>. You feel held, <u>safe</u>, no need to go anywhere else.

Comments: The <u>safe</u> aspect of the afterlife environment is important (and mentioned elsewhere in esoteric literature)—*unlike our sojourn on earth. A major reason I guess (there are others), is that once one becomes a discarnate, one is fully aware of one's <u>immortality</u>—as scientifically covered in my book. (Ref: 8). Duffy's teaching here gives a good validating picture of what to expect. Elsewhere it seems there is also some descriptive "new information."*

Question No 12

Terri: Do you realize you have died right away?

Duffy: No. You don't realize it right away. You feel the same as on Earth but you slowly start to notice that things are not "life" as you knew it. It's a little strange, at first, but there are people there you love to reassure you. You are so happy to see them that you forget the life you just came from. You keep acclimating to the new life. As you do, you realize you like it and so there is no fear.

Comments: Same as above, but here, the critical factor is that in an afterlife— "<u>there is no fear</u>" and <u>this is an important validating factor</u> (Ref: same as Q11 above.).

Question No 13

Terri: Do you remember the life you came from when you first pass?

Duffy: It seems like a faint knowing. But there is no "past" here. So, the life you "came" from is a part of oneself and seen as such here. But not like, "Oh I just left that life."

Comments: Interesting comment and perhaps "new information"—in the sense that Duffy feels one's past is just a continuation of one's "time" line, but in the case of himself—as a "discarnate", since there is no such thing as "time" for them—it becomes just part of their "event line." <u>This</u>

<u>*therefore is very validating*</u> *(And covered in detail in my book). Also, it reinforces the concept that past and future as time-based concepts <u>for us, are but earth "illusions."</u> But they are very obvious to a discarnate—who can freely travel to the past or future, in <u>space,</u> not time!* (Ref. 9)

Question No 14

Terri: Do you miss your loved ones when you first pass?

Duffy: You feel their pain from separating from you. You feel your loved one's thoughts. You know them. We want to give something like hope to our loved ones. We want to say, "I'm here!" We try to give <u>signs we know might work</u>. They are clever and have meaning for the loved one. We try and reach you through your heart wisdom. No, it does not upset us if you can't receive. <u>We are one with whatever IS</u>. When we feel an openness, a light then we try again. Different souls can connect in different ways. It kind of goes with their personality. Like, I was very physical so I prefer touch.

<u>Comments:</u> *Interesting but not evidential. Duffy says, "We try to give signs we know might work"—possibly synchronicities?—Terri claims many such experiences. Again, Duffy stresses "Oneness." The <u>methodology mentioned here by Duffy in contacting us humans is interesting</u> and possibly new information.* (No Ref.)

Question No 15

Terri: Is there such thing as a soulmate?

Duffy: No, not a soul mate. There are many companions or other aspects to us that could be considered "mates." These aspects complement whatever is needed in the current life-path growth stage chosen. <u>So, a soul mate is a human term</u>. But really it should be said as the mates of the soul! They appear to us to reflect what we are ready to learn. These mates of the soul are the facets of a diamond, to use an analogy. <u>We are all facets of the one diamond</u>. All part of the one diamond soul light. All facets mirror and reflect each other and growth lessons being learned. In a way, every person in your life is a soul mate. An important mate to your core soul. <u>No person is of greater or lesser importance to you. All mates have needed gifts for us.</u> Comments: ***Excellent new information*** *which rings with truth. Again, there is a reiteration that* <u>*all friends and others*</u> **are one** <u>*with us*</u>—*using an interesting analogy of a* <u>*diamond of many facets (the diamond of course being God!)*</u>. *But Duffy also says,* "*All mates have needed gifts for us*"—*We are being taught in a very clear way by Duffy that everyone we meet is* <u>*important and equal*</u>. *Wonderfully validating for both Duffy and Terri. And well supported by Jane Roberts'* "*Seth*" *teachings.* (Ref 10)

Question No 17

Terri: From your perspective, what is death?

Duffy: Well, sis, death is a step. A step into another space. It is like going from the sidewalk to the grass…it feels different but more natural. Better than natural really. <u>Death is nothing to fear</u>. It is just a state of being…we have all that is needed here. <u>Anything you can imagine is real or possible in death</u>. <u>False claims by people are that death is a place of judgment or punishment.</u> <u>There is only possibility</u>. I want you to know that I am NOT DEAD. I am alive in another realm. <u>I have a life here with purpose and meaning.</u> <u>Eternity is a way of saying life goes on and in any way one needs.</u> All it takes is imagining. <u>Using your mind to make it so</u>. There is guidance for the expansion. <u>A loving presence is available always</u>. I am not lonely. I am not alone. I am on my way at all times and in all moments.

<u>Comments:</u> *Wonderfully* <u>*inspiring*</u> *and helpful, But, covered elsewhere fully in other esoteric literature, particularly Dr Michael Newton's books,*

(Ref: 11). *Not really new information, but strongly evidential for Terri and Duffy.*

Question No 18

Terri: Is there such thing as <u>evil or harmful spirits who have not died or are attaching themselves to humans?</u>

Duffy: <u>No there is no such thing as evil here!</u> That is a <u>man-made concept. Evil is a concept that comes from an impure state of mind</u> and here all states of mind are pure. <u>I don't mean to be mean and say impure is bad. It is just tinted with the fears of earthly life</u> that's all.

<u>Comment:</u> *Contrary to belief by many, Duffy is dogmatically denying Terri's question involving evil or harmful spirits attaching themselves to humans—which may well be correct. The reason being, "We create our own reality"—for which there is strong <u>experimental</u> evidence. (Ref:12) A **practical** (<u>non-experimental</u>) example of belief influencing ourselves is reported instances of "Stigmata." Probably "new information"—as this seems this is one of mankind's many "illusions" while on earth, but not a factor believed or experienced "upstairs"—as Duffy teaches. Note: Ghosts and poltergeists are no doubt valid and real for us humans, but not "possession" as presumably inferred by Duffy. (See further comments below.)*

<u>Duffy Cont.</u> Once a spirit has ended its earth mission, so to speak, it fully detaches and goes on to another form chosen. <u>It is not possible to stay connected to a human. It takes too much vibration energy needed to move on. When we reach out and touch you that is momentary and we can sustain it. But once in spirit essence here, we have only momentary energy or vibration to connect with the earth layer.</u> Seems "new information/knowledge". <u>So, no, evil is not present in any spirit on this side. Evil is a concept of the mind and reflects needed growth lessons. Those who believe in evil spirits have a lesson to</u>

learn about goodness, I guess, or something around that concept. Most likely learning to make a choice in themselves whether to act for the good or not. Comments Cont. *Duffy's teaching that a spirit <u>cannot maintain prolonged attachment to a human</u> seems particularly useful and "new knowledge" as, importantly, it rules out misguided belief in <u>permanent</u> "possession" by another entity. It appears that such a belief is probably a false "medieval" concept. Think Voodoo beliefs and "exorcisms"—where people react as a form of <u>self-hypnosis</u> (see "Seth" teachings,* Ref:13*). Those who consider they are possessed by an evil spirit (while believing this completely), may falsely, although unwittingly, portray all the symptoms they witness based on watching and mimicking the behavior of others with the same false beliefs. Classically, this was a behavior phenomenon observed repeatedly during the famous Salem 1692 witch trials. Psychiatrists consistently identify all this as "hysterical behavior," <u>not possession</u>. "Possession" is said to occur legitimately <u>but temporarily</u> by higher entities in cases of deep trance mediums, but said consistently by such mediums, cannot occur without their permission. So, Duffy's teachings here certainly support this, and therefore would also seem excellent "new knowledge."*

Question No 20 (a)

Terri: Is Information a fundamental factor in Nature?

Duffy: Yes, information is carried throughout the universe by waves of harmonized energy. <u>Information does not guarantee an outcome, though. It just is. It exists in various forms for the "viewer."</u>

Comments: Duffy's phrase "harmonized energy" is another way (perhaps better!) of saying "resonance"—which brilliantly agrees with PCAR *quantum hologram communication science (Ref 14). What <u>follows</u> below (and underlined), I feel must apply only though to Duffy and readily to all discarnates—as most humans cannot normally freely channel information/*

knowledge—*only medium/psychics such as Terri who can readily source this information.*

Duffy Cont. The consciousness or eyes looks for what is needed and sees the information that can be accommodated into the viewing consciousness seamlessly. As the viewer seeks answers to grow in consciousness, so the information most "fitting," is seen or chosen. The viewer assimilates the information in a way that keeps equilibrium. Information feeds growth. All kinds of growth happens simultaneously all over the universe in this way.

Comments Cont. *The above is* **new information** *on how information/knowledge is obtained freely from the universe by psychics/mediums (and discarnates), and agrees very much with the whole of the chapter 9 Annex in my book.* (Ref:15) *The concept that "information feeds (spiritual) growth, seems very apt and is very much supported by the amount of learning that is necessary upstairs in "cluster groups" plus multiple reincarnations.*

Question No 20 (b)

Terri: Where does information come from?

Duffy: It comes from the sea of possibility. No joke! The sea is the source of all matter. The sea holds and carries information.

Comments: *The "Sea of possibility"—seems an odd description, but valid! It is better known as the Zero-point field or Akashic field. A sea/foam of virtual particles coming into and disappearing from existence, which surround all matter. So, the above is spot on and verified/validated as correct in terms of considerable science support. Excellent!* (Ref:16)

Question No 21

Terri: Where does the sea come from?

Duffy: It has always been and there is no beginning or ending. Those are human concepts.

Comment: *Seems correct—and important* **new information** *by suggesting it has always existed. Conventional scientific wisdom is that our existence, life itself and consciousness followed consequently from the Big Bang. But this says otherwise. Whether we accept this or not—it nevertheless <u>conforms</u> to quantum mechanics that shows at a quantum level <u>time</u> does not exist. (Ref:17) So, this seems correct! Again, validity for both Terri and Duffy is maintained.*

Question No 22

Terri: How do matter particles acquire mass?

Duffy: Matter particles acquire mass through a strange kind of osmosis. The particles get their bulk from complex fields of thought form.

Comment: *Elsewhere said as the result of intent and thought, matter consolidates from virtual particles <u>which exist in the zero-point Field</u>. (Ref: 18)*

<u>Duffy Cont.</u> These are gained in strength and structure through thought-form variables. Not all particles are the same. Mass depends on a balance of information and need to expend density outward. The more density required, the less regular the mass-form. <u>Mass cannot be self sustained</u>. It requires likeminded force combined with gravitational pull to keep it in balance.

Comments: *Elsewhere, it is said occasional observation/thought in an afterlife is needed to sustain created matter otherwise it would eventually disappear. (cannot recall reference—I think Michael Newton's books). All this is probably both correct and helpful.*

Probably New Information

Question No 24

Terri: Is there a Multi-Verse that our universe comes from?

Duffy: No, no multi-verse here dear (that your universe comes from), only vast reaches of space and time that are varied in complexity and formulated differently. By that I mean that all universes come about independently of each other. They all arose in a complex soup. Some are younger than others. Some are vast in size and shape. Others small comparatively. The idea of the multi-verse has its origins in man's need to know where this all started.

It didn't start really. Rather it has been evolving forever. Time is the key. Our time here belies a start and a finish. We have always just been here and universes have been growing forever and always will.

<u>Comment Cont.</u> *Because in non-physical reality there is no time (nice and simple!). (Ref: 19)*

<u>Duffy Cont.</u> There is no end. Your universe is small. It has special properties to allow life as you know it on Earth. Other universes give rise to other types of life. They are all a part of the great puzzle.

<u>Comment Cont.</u> *Most of this sounds like* **new knowledge** *i.e. the cosmology of many universes and "all arising in a complex soup", our universe being quite small etc. Has a ring of truth to it, but I do not know of any scientific supporting evidence—except the theory of a massive quantum fluctuation occasionally giving birth to a new universe—as an unproven but nevertheless a quite believable <u>theory (sadly though without evidence).</u>*

Question No 25

Terri: What about the nature of time?

<u>Comment:</u> *Importantly I believe that what follows as Duffy's response is him talking about physical reality. Not his non-physical reality environment, where time does not exist. The distinction is very important.*

Duffy: Time does travel, but in a way that is different than we think of. It travels by way of heat and light.

Heat and light create a kind of vacuum. A sort of suction that pulls time forward or back. The vacuum is "alive." It has information so it works to give the most beneficial movement to create a time situation. Because time is the glue that holds everything together, it adapts to make the closest structure the most comfortable, like a mother cradling a baby. Time supports atoms—it receives communication from them about what is needed for support. Time is conscious. Again, like time mirrors the consciousness of the planet like a mother mirrors her infant. It gives the planet a sense of self. There are multitudes of ways for consciousness to grow and to know itself that are available in other time situations—other galaxies, planets, stars.

Time bends and is circular. Time isn't one linear thing or just one place. It goes all over—all directions and changes as needed to adapt to the particular star or galaxy conditions. Time is flexible and adaptable. It fulfills a purpose. It is the invisible glue that keeps everything together.

Take Earth, for example. On Earth, consciousness is related to time. There is a direct connection. <u>On Earth growth is measured according to time;</u> on other galaxies, growth is completely differently measured as time operates differently there.

Souls can learn more by choosing to go to different galaxies. The speed of light affects time too. It slows it down or speeds it up. Heat can bend time. As you get closer to the sun, time compresses and condenses.

*<u>Comment Cont.</u> Again, this seems like completely **new knowledge** throughout and has a ring of truth to it. It also seems internally consistent. The concept*

that the vacuum (any such vacuum, comprises the zero-point field is filled with virtual subatomic particles) is alive, is supported by "solid" science: called "panpsychicism": See (Ref: 20)

WORLD

*Folded like origami inside the tiny white planet of
hard moonflower seed
unseen multitudes of vine, stem and tightly packed
blossom heavy with contained scent and anticipation,
knowing already to wait for dusk,
for the secret lunar signal;
the summer night's new bud shivers its
first infinitesimal release, enough only to taste
the earth's gasp of cool relief
rising damp off the lawn.
A drop of twilight slips into the pursed mouth;
membranes hum with the vibration of peepers
singing in the trees. Night lures and teases
till the single pod, overcome,
surrenders like a lover.
Luminous petals thick and fresh as clean linen,
unwind themselves to stretch,
spread wide in thrall
to the mirror of the moon's high face.
I hold it all in my palm.*

—Melissa Cumber

Afterword

Communication with the deceased *is* possible! The good news is that current views about death and the afterlife are quickly being transformed. I and many others sense that a paradigm shift in this regard is imminent.

The number of people worldwide who have experienced after-death communications now numbers in the millions. Many people have reported spontaneous connections and communications—without asking for or seeking them. Others seek connection through such avenues as mediums, electronic voice phenomena, or the pendulum method. Connection with one's loved ones who have "crossed over" is not guaranteed, but there is a way to make oneself as open and ready as possible. We already have what we need—our loving hearts and open minds!

My journey through grief has made me a much more confident and peaceful person. I believe without a doubt that my relationship with Duffy continues to this day. I continue to spend time with him often, although not necessarily daily now. Our new relationship has many facets—through meditation, automatic writing, dreams, the pendulum, visualization, and touch. I have the feeling and hope that in this new connection to Duffy, I am simultaneously helping myself and his spirit to reach a new level; he in his new world and I, here in mine.

What happens after we die is still a mystery; but maybe we have more of a window to the other side than we realize. Through grief's journey I have come to believe that life is eternal—not in a way I can tangibly know—but in a way that will reveal itself after I die. Through the death of my brother and the after-death communications we have had, I now know that I am loved and that there is nothing to fear—either on this earth or after I depart from this earthly plane. As endless spirits on a magnificent journey, we are riding eternity's light. Love is the water we swim in and we are each a piece of God; a blessing, a gift.

Duffy wants us to know that much of what has been written by those who have had near-death experiences or have had visits from their deceased loved ones is real!

Regarding our soul's purpose here on earth, he wishes to say the following:

First and most importantly, we are all eternal beings and the ground of all existence is love. Each soul is a splintering off of the one, pure, highest or divine love. Whether we call this divine love, "God" or some other name doesn't matter.

Life and death are but two points on an endless wave. Souls are born and die in their successive manifested lives repeatedly and eternally. This is so they can learn the lessons needed for each new incarnation. The main task of each soul is the development of its capacity for love! All souls are destined to return back to divine love eventually, once their capacity for love has reached its fullest reflection of Divinity.

A soul can choose to reincarnate here on Earth or anywhere in the universe in order to learn the lessons it chooses for itself. A soul chooses to come to Earth in order to learn the unique lessons that

Afterword

can only be found here. Each soul comes to this planet with a plan and in perfect form. All of the potential to learn its lessons is contained within this human personality.

Yes, there is free will! Our choices shape our lives, but in the end all roads lead to fulfilling our purpose here. We can't help but learn the lessons we came here to learn. Even those whose lives are cut short, through external circumstances or through suicide, have learned their lessons and chosen one of the exit points available and agreed upon ahead of time. There is no such thing as failure in the grand plan; only choice.

It is not easy to be a human and souls know this when they agree to come here. But even though the challenges are great, the rewards are greater!

When any soul does choose to take on a human existence, it takes on the challenges of having a personality and a body as well as emotions and feelings. All souls undergo similar challenges, though in different ways. Each unique human life will present as many different ways to learn and master the challenges of being a human as there are incarnate spirits.

These challenges are mastered through trial and error. To make mistakes is a good thing. With each mistake comes the ability to reflect and choose more wisely the next time—and to grow in wisdom.

Over time, it is essential to develop a "wise self" as opposed to a "smart self." The wise self learns to develop his or her spiritual capacity. This means developing a positive connection to the divine principles of love and service. This capacity is developed by finding time to reflect, pray, visualize and speak positively, spending time in nature and learning to listen to nature's messages and rhythms. Most importantly, the "wise self" puts service to others and care for the earth as its priority over individual needs.

Our first challenge is to build our capacity for more love. In order to let increasing amounts of love in, we must master our fears. Our fears are not real—they are like paper tigers—designed to distract us from our own wisdom. As we develop our wise selves and as we live our lives more and more based on divine principles such as respect and dignity for all, our fears transform into fuel to help us continue onward.

Our second challenge is to create and seek peace wherever possible. Whether it be in one's own heart, mind, or in relating to others, cultivating peace is essential to our growth. When we face our own fears we are better able to live in peace. Violence of all kinds reflects the lack of peace humans have developed within themselves. Violent acts will continue and even increase if we do not develop our peaceful ways. War and violence around the world will continue until there is more cooperation between nations.

Whenever faced with a choice, people must learn to choose cooperation over competition. In many ways healthy competition is a good thing, but cooperation is the glue of mankind. In fact, without it the human species will not survive.

The third challenge is to remove judgement from our minds. When we die, we are not judged by a god sitting on high. We are only judged by our own selves. We face the consequences of our choices and we decide which form to take on next in order to continue our growth. Our fear of being judged by others and by our own self judgement clouds the truth of our own heart. Humans must make their heart's wisdom the primary thing.

The fourth and most important challenge is to acknowledge that our world is at risk. Even more problematic and damaging than the threat of nuclear war is the destruction of our planet's delicate ecosystem. We are at a crossroads. The most serious threat to humankind is climate change. We have already done serious damage, but

Afterword

it still can be reversed. We must make caring for our earth and all living creatures a priority over materialism.

Finally, the dead are in fact very much in existence, but existing at a different vibration. Free of earthly attachments, they are able to choose how they want to progress. They care deeply about the living and want to continue their connection with us. Not all of them are able to do so, but many can. They want the living to know that they are always with us and for us to remain hopeful and keep looking ahead. They want us to have faith! From the perspective of eternity, all is given and all is possible.

We don't need any special devices or so-called experts to help us keep our connection. We don't need permission or approval. All we need is our desire. An open heart and the courage to keep trusting ourselves is all we need to keep our love alive.

Appendix 1
Basic Types of After-Death Communications (ADCs)

The following are brief descriptions of the most commonly experienced types of after-death communications people report having with their discarnate loved ones. A person can have one or more types of ADCs—either at the same time or at different times. ADCs can take place anywhere and at any time. Two or more people who are together at the same place and at the same time may share an ADC experience.

It is very common to have the themes of these contacts be about comfort, reassurance, and hope. ADC can be experienced by parents, spouses, siblings, children, other family members, and friends. It seems that the discarnate want their loved ones to know they still exist and that you will be reunited with them when you leave your life here on Earth. They assure us that they will be there to meet us and even to assist us as we make our own transition at death.

1. **Visual ADC:** There are many kinds of visual appearances, which can be divided into partial "sightings" and full visual sightings. Types of sightings include: a milky or misty shape,

solid, opaque, outlines of a whole body or just the head and shoulders or faces surrounded by color. Heads and shoulders of the loved one are common as are sightings near or at the foot of the bed.

2. **Auditory ADC:** People report they can hear an external voice with their ears or they get communications by telepathy, hearing the voice in their "mind." Some people can have two-way communications through telepathy. Voices are easily identifiable as the loved one and usually relay messages of comfort and assurance that they (the deceased) are fine.

   Some people hear a phone ringing, and when they answer it, their deceased loved ones give a message. Two-way conversations have also been reported. The discarnate loved one's voice is usually clear and can sound close or distant. Sometimes, when the call on a physical phone is over there will not be an obvious hang up sound or dial tone. People report getting these calls on both cell and land lines. Some people engage in the practice of Electronic Voice Recognition (EVR) by using a computer or recorder or even a phone to hear their discarnate loved one's voice.

3. **Tactile ADC:** Usually those who have had a very close physical and emotional relationship with a loved one will receive the familiar touch of that person. People report feeling touch on a hand, shoulder, and/or the top of the head that gives comfort and reassurance. Most common types of touch are a caress, a kiss, a gentle pat, squeeze of the hand, or even a hug.

4. **Olfactory ADC:** Many people smell their loved ones favorite perfume, after shave, or even bath soap. Other typical smells

Appendix 1

are: favorite foods, tobacco smoke, or their personal scent. Often the smells appear when a grieving person is thinking about their loved one.

5. **Sentient ADC:** This is the most common form of contact. It is a feeling that your loved one is nearby, even though they cannot be seen or heard. It is a sense of the person that is felt—their personality, expressions, and mannerisms.

6. **Visitation or Vision ADC:** You may see a deceased loved one right after you wake up or while asleep, in a picture that can be either two or three dimensional. People report seeing these vivid, clear visions externally, with their eyes open, or internally, in the mind. Often communication of this kind happens during meditation. When this happens during sleep it is called a "dream visitation."

7. **Unusual Electrical or Physical ADC:** It is often reported that a wide variety of physical signs from the discarnate come through immediately after death and even years later. Such signs could be lights or lamps flickering, radios, stereos, and tvs spontaneously turning on and other mechanical objects becoming activated. Some people have reported that photographs or other objects associated with the discarnate are moved. They might be knocked over or even move to another part of the home.

8. **Out-Of-Body ADC:** These most often happen when you are in a relaxed meditative state. They are very specific experiences during which you feel yourself leave your physical body. You might visit your loved one in a place nearby or at some other place. It might be on Earth and it might be in another part of the universe. It could be in a spiritual

dimension that we might call "heaven." Many people report that these experiences bring a feeling of deep peace and connection with their loved ones.

9. **Synchronistic Symbols, Events, and Signs** ADC: Many people receive these by requesting them to appear and for others they occur spontaneously. These signs might be subtle or not so subtle. They can easily be discounted as mere coincidences and not realized to be signs from their loved ones. The most common signs include feathers, repeating numbers, butterflies, animals, flowers, rainbows, and objects that were personally meaningful or related to the discarnate loved one.

Appendix 2
The Science Behind Mediumistic and Psychic Communication with Discarnates and Gaining Knowledge from the Universe

> *"You are a non-physical consciousness that is experiencing physical reality."*
> —Bashar

The following article is a revised version of a Preface written by Professor Ervin Laszlo and Gyorglyi Szabo to the book "Earth's Cosmic Ascendancy" by George E. Moss. This Foreword has been slightly revised by A. B. Scott-Hill, author of the science book, "The Paranormal is Normal," aimed at making it more understandable to the layman, and minor updating in accordance with recent science developments.

Terminology used:

Nonlocal: This is a science term used to distinguish non-physical (i.e. quantum type) communication concerned with paranormal phenomena (such as telepathy, dowsing etc.) which is unrelated to distance, and has been shown by experiment to occur virtually instantaneously.

Coherence: (Physics definition) A fixed relationship between the phase of waves in a beam of radiation of a single frequency.

1.0 Non-physical reality and science.

"The mysteries of out-of-body and near-death experiences and of the experience of "receiving" as a medium—channeled messages from discarnates, or "receiving" information/knowledge—as a psychic "from the universe;" arises from people being unfamiliar with the plethora of non-physical forms of existence. Most people currently are not ready to accept that such experiences are real. Therefore, just as we have to study the laws applicable to material reality (Newtonian and Einsteinian physics); here, with non-physical reality—it is necessary to study the laws of non-physical science which comprises quantum physics, the laws applicable to the very small, i.e. subatomic particles.

2.0 Communication from Non-Physical reality by Resonance

One such law is the transmission of information by resonance. We know that information is transferred between mingling quantum wave-fields when the waves are in phase and attain coherence—they are then said to "conjugate," or exhibit resonance. Every single thing in the universe has its own resonance; every single human being has its own quantum vibration. Everything and every human exchange of information occurs when its emanating quantum waves are in phase with another person, or entity (which even includes thoughts or information). Then they are said to <u>resonate</u> together.

Our brain and body receive millions of resonances every day, but we fail to decode them and hence we do not actively resonate with them. Perception is highly selective. The way we filter the information that reaches us, is determined by the traits of our upbringing, the influences that act on us and our particular belief system.

Mediums and psychics can process information that "normal" people filter out. This information is anomalous for most people and unperceived; it is nonlocal information based on quantum-level resonance. When one processes information in this mode, quantum communicated signals, images, insights and intuition reach conscious awareness.

3.0 The Quantum Holographic Universe, where everything at a quantum level is interconnected.

The experience of mediums/psychics prompts us to revise the classical concept of perception of the world. Our world is not a vast machine reducible to its individual parts, but a holographically integrated irreducible whole. The modern mind, influenced by classical physics, filters out information that does not mesh with its materialistic, machine-like preconceptions. Modern people believe only what is perceptible to their senses—the restricted perception of just what they can see and hear and touch. Anything that is not sense-perceptible they consider but an illusion or delusion. The dominant belief system places mind and consciousness in the category of unreal things, because there is a mind-set that mind and consciousness are not material, or physical, and wrongly that they simply do not exist.

The simplest way for the modern mind to deal with them is to wrongly claim both that they are produced by the material brain—and as a by-product of complex cerebral functioning. Consciousness researchers now realize, however, that this assertion without evidence does not answer the question regarding where the mind and consciousness in the world are located, because it cannot tell us how something as material as the brain could produce something as immaterial as a thought, a perception, an intuition, a sensation, or a volition.

4.0 The Mind-Brain Conundrum.

The above is the "hard question" of consciousness research, and it turned out to be not only hard but intractable. That we cannot say how the brain would produce consciousness, does not mean that the brain would not "have" consciousness. It could have it not as its product, but as something it receives, elaborates, conserves, and transmits. There is more evidence speaking to this concept of consciousness, than to the consciousness-as-by-product-of-the-brain assumption. Yet the argument that dominates the modern mind is that consciousness is a product of the brain, because when the brain stops functioning, consciousness stops as well. This, however, is like claiming that our TV set produces the programs it displays, because when we shut off our set, the display ceases. Evidently the program—more exactly, the electromagnetic wave-patterns that reach the antenna and through it the set that displays the program—continues to exist.

In the same way consciousness can continue to exist when the brain has died—when it is "shut off." We do not suggest that the contents of consciousness are "produced" ready made by some extra-somatic intelligence, only that the phenomena of consciousness—our direct experience of the world—is the consequence of our brain's reception of signals that originate beyond it.

They originate in the consciousness that pervades the universe—in the "spirit world" that spiritual entities speak about. We receive signals from this world from the vantage point of our brain—from our being-in-the-world. This is what constitutes our conscious experience. It is not limited to one point in space and time, because consciousness is nonlocal in the universe.

Human consciousness displays this element of nonlocality: it persists also beyond the brain. There is good evidence on this score in NDEs (near-death experiences), in OBEs (out-of-body experiences), and even in experiences transmitted by electronic instruments (in EVPs, electronic voice phenomena). Why should we not consider the evidence for medium-transmitted messages in the same way? The difference between NDEs, OBEs and messages transmitted by mediums is that information in NDEs and OBEs is received by the subjects themselves, and with medium-transmitted experiences, it is received by the mediums. The process is likely to be the same.

The veracity of reports by people who claim they died as the result of an accident or some other cause, but then came back (or were sent back) appear more credible because in NDEs those making the claims experienced the events they recount themselves. We doubt the experiences conveyed by mediums because we suspect that the mediums could be making up their reports, whether voluntarily or involuntarily, as fraud or hoax, or as the result of subconscious suggestion by others. Yet there are well documented cases where the mediums convey information they could not have obtained by ordinary means, and where they recount experiences they could not possibly have undergone themselves. Where did they get this information, and how did they come by these experiences? The answer can only be framed by the concept of consciousness that is, and has always been, affirmed by great prophets, artists, and spiritual people—but also consistently and repeatedly by channeled nonhuman entities.

5.0 Entanglement and the Zero-point Field.

If we take an in-depth and unbiased look at the evidence, and seek the explanation for it in reference to the latest discoveries of the sciences, we come to the conclusion that the information we access in the universe is not a mosaic of unrelated bits and pieces, floating randomly in space and time. It is an integrated whole, where all parts are instantly and intrinsically related to all other parts. The consciousness that we access—in which we participate—is a hologram. In it all things are "entangled" in space as well as in time. This is no longer an esoteric tenet: it is a conclusion derived from the latest findings of contemporary quantum physics. In the surrounding quantum field at absolute zero in the cosmos—in what we call the "zero" point field, which surrounds all of us and everything comprising virtual subatomic particles (or Akasha, an ancient name for this)—there is no space and no time; space and time are its perceivable, measurable manifestations. The deep dimension creates physical space-time, but it is not "in" space-time. This was an esoteric insight a few years ago; it is a scientific fact today. We should view the information conveyed by trance mediums and other mediums particularly spiritually advanced to channel information/knowledge in light of these emerging insights.

Could they not have accessed some elements of the holographically integrated information that pervades the universe? And could the information they have accessed not have originated anywhere in space-time? The answer is yes: this is entirely possible. There is yet another factor that calls for our attention in regard to the credibility of the messages conveyed by mediums. Are the entities they channel physically real? By "physically real" we do not mean that they are material, for the physics we have in mind is not classical but quantum physics. Reality in light of quantum physics is not material; it is quantum-informational. Our body and brain are one particular kind of configuration of quantum-information, and quanta on the one hand and galaxies on the other are other configurations. They appear as material entities because they have particular locations in space and time and produce measurable effect on interaction. But there are entities in the universe that do not have these qualities, yet merit being considered real entities: for example, quantum field excitations at the Planck-scale. These are photons and other particles without rest-mass. Non-physical entities claim to be constituted of photons: if such an entity constituted essentially of light, they could be just as real as a quantum configuration based on the integration of quanta into atoms, of atoms into molecules, of molecules into cells, and of cells into biological organisms with brains. When we hear/channel a non-physical entity speaking to us, we witness one kind of quantum-configuration (perhaps with the appearance and characteristic of an orb of light), communicating with another (human) kind. That this communication involves vast distances in space is not an anomaly. In a quantum-entangled space-time all things are instantly connected. The entity could be sending his messages from next door, or from another galaxy. As long as the entity is in the same physical space-time, his messages reach us instantly.

6.0 Thoughts, Information and Knowledge.

Thought, as channeled by so called advanced non-human entities advise that "thoughts" are the most powerful thing in the universe. Thoughts are powerful because they are coherent information, and the universe is built of information. When the information is assembled by an information configured entity into coherent messages that "inform" other information configured entities, they create (as David Bohm would say) "effective information."

Valid channeled (and psychically derived) messages/information are powerful messages if they are not filtered out. but consciously "received." Whether accurate and valid is up to the reader to check—as well as they can, as advanced entities advise "testing" (and the Bible) for consistency etc. Consciously receptive readers can be effectively informed by messages whether they come from human or psychically derived directly channeled information/knowledge obtained from what is considered the source of the "universe" store of all knowledge and event memory of all that has ever happened—the zero-point field (Akashic field).

January 2014 (amended in 2017)

7.0 Consciousness

Ervin Laszlo also proposes that the quantum vacuum zero-point field—which is thought to contain all the event information of our history from the Big Bang to now—is also consciousness. Everything in the universe therefore has consciousness; from a pebble to a tree, to a cloud, to a person (known as panpsychicism). While this goes against the view of mainstream science, there are some highly respected scientists such as Freeman Dyson, David Bohm and Fritjof Capra, who support the idea that the universe is in fact conscious. Ervin Laszlo says that life happens because it comes from the quantum vacuum.

What is consciousness? Consciousness is about being aware of our own existence and the environment in which we live. So, if one sub-atomic particle reacts in line with another particle somewhere else in the universe, we could say it is aware of what the other one is doing. In a way, it is aware of itself in the universe. So, the question is: Is it enough to say all particles in the universe are conscious?

We are conscious of our existence and have evolved a brain able to access and use the consciousness held in the quantum vacuum

Appendix 2

which envelops everything. Consciousness is yet another manifestation of coherence allowing a mass of nerve cells to co-operate and form a unified sense of self.

NOTE: Scientist Professor Ervin Laszlo, who wrote this article, holds the highest degree of the Sorbonne (State Doctorate) plus four honorary Doctorates. He is founder and president of the international think tank "Club of Budapest." He is also head of the "General Evolution Research Group," and has published more than 70 books and in excess of 400 papers. He is the recipient of the 2001 Goi Award, (Japanese Peace Prize) and has twice been the nominee for the Nobel Peace Prize.

References

Q1 Ref 1: *The Paranormal is Normal (The Science Validation to Reincarnation, The Paranormal and your Immortality)*, by A.B. Scott-Hill, Pg. 183
Ref 2: ibid., Pg. 261
Ref 3: *Afterlife Teaching from Stephen the Martyr*, by Rev, Michael Cocks Pg,13, Also Biblical References: John 10:30,38 also 17:11,21 Galatians 3:26,28 Romans 12:5 Colossians 3:11 Corinthians 1:12.
Ref 4: *The Paranormal is Normal (The Science Validation to Reincarnation, The Paranormal and your Immortality)*, by A.B. Scott-Hill, Pg.169–180, but encapsulated by reading all of Part 1.

Q2 Ref 5: For "intent", see Ibid, Pg. 58, 70. Also, *The Conscious Universe*, by Dean Radin. Pg. 143. For, "The Zero-point field," see *The Paranormal is Normal (The Science Validation to Reincarnation, The Paranormal and your Immortality)*, by A.B. Scott-Hill, Pg. 60 and the book *The God Theory: Universes, Zero-point Fields, and What's Behind It All"*, by astrophysicist Bernard Haisch.

Q3 Ref 6: *The Paranormal is Normal (The Science Validation to Reincarnation, The Paranormal and your Immortality)*, by A.B. Scott-Hill Pg. 259.

Q4 Ref: 7: ibid, Pg. 128

Q7, Q8, Q9, Q10—see text, no specific references.

Q11	Ref 8: ibid, Pg. 257
Q12	Ref 8: same as Q11 above
Q13	Ref 9: ibid Pgs. 104–111
Q14	No reference.
Q15	Ref 10: ibid Pg. 154
Q16	Omitted
Q17	Ref 11: ibid Pgs.257–262
Q18	Ref 12: ibid Pg. 45–46
	Ref 13: "The Nature of Personal Reality: by Jane Roberts, Pgs. 362,363,508
Q19	Omitted
Q20a	Ref 14: The Paranormal is Normal (The Science Validation to Reincarnation, The Paranormal and your Immortality), by A.B. Scott-Hill Pgs. 74–79, Ref 15: ibid Pgs. 271–292
Q20b	Ref 16: ibid Pgs. 60–62
Q21	Ref 17: ibid Pgs. 104–111
Q22	Ref 18: *Earth's Cosmic Ascendency*—by George Moss. Kindle Loc.190.
Q23	Omitted
Q24	Ref 19: same as Q21
Q25	Ref 20: *The Paranormal is Normal (The Science Validation to Reincarnation, The Paranormal and your Immortality)*, by A.B. Scott-Hill, Pg. 41

About the Author

Ms. Segal has been a licensed Marriage and Family Therapist specializing in Art therapy for over 14 years.

She has worked with children and families on healing trauma, grief and loss and abuse. She is an accomplished artist in the mediums of jewelry design, photography and painting. She currently lives in beautiful Northern California.

www.ingramcontent.com/pod-product-compliance
Lightning Source LLC
Chambersburg PA
CBHW070609300426
44113CB00010B/1469